Autumn

Recipes Inspired by Nature's Bounty

Time-Life Books is a division of Time Life Inc.
Time-Life is a trademark of Time Warner Inc. U.S.A.

TIME-LIFE CUSTOM PUBLISHING
Vice President and Publisher: Terry Newell
Associate Publisher: Teresa Hartnett
Managing Editor: Donia Ann Steele
Director of New Product Development: Quentin McAndrew
Director of Sales: Neil Levin
Director of Financial Operations: J. Brian Birky

WILLIAMS-SONOMA
Founder/Vice-Chairman: Chuck Williams
Book Buyer: Victoria Kalish

Produced by
WELDON OWEN INC.
President: John Owen
Vice President and Publisher: Wendely Harvey
Chief Financial Officer: Larry Partington
Associate Publisher: Lisa Chaney Atwood
Consulting Editor: Norman Kolpas
Copy Editor: Sharon Silva
Production Director: Stephanie Sherman
Production Manager: Jen Dalton
Production Editor: Katherine Withers Cobbs
Design: Angela Williams
Food Photographer: Penina
Food and Prop Stylist: Pouké
Assistant Food Photographer: Martin Dunham
Assistant Food Stylist: Michelle Syracuse
Illustrations: Thorina Rose
Co-Editions Director: Derek Barton

Manufactured by Toppan Printing Co., (H.K.) Ltd.
Printed in China

First Printing 1997
10 9 8 7 6 5 4 3 2 1

Library of Congress
Cataloging-in-Publication Data:

Weir, Joanne
    Autumn : recipes inspired by nature's bounty / Joanne Weir.
        p. cm. -- (Williams-Sonoma seasonal celebration)
    Includes index.
    ISBN 0-7835-4608-4
    1. Cookery. 2. Autumn. I. Title. II. Series.
TX714.W333 1997
641.5'64--DC20   96-35503
                                                        CIP

A Note on Weights and Measures:
All recipes include customary U.S. and metric measurements.
Metric conversions are based on a standard developed for these
books and have been rounded off. Actual weights may vary.

Autumn

Recipes Inspired by Nature's Bounty

Joanne Weir

Autumn

Autumn's abundant and varied nut crops lend rich flavor and texture to seasonal dishes.

Winter squashes have hard protective shells that make them ideal for storing into the coming season.

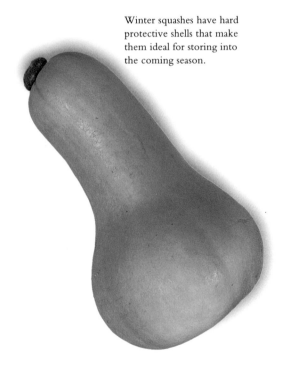

The cornucopia endures as the symbol of autumn with good reason. At this time of year, garden plots and market stalls alike overflow with an abundant harvest that was first coaxed to life by the summer sun. Hard-shelled squashes, the season's most bounteous crop, delight with their harlequin array of shapes, sizes and colors. Boughs hang heavy with a wonderful variety of apples and pears. Beneath the cover of fallen leaves, wild mushrooms push upward. The cool, sheltering ground transforms the starch of roots, tubers and onions to a sublime sweetness. Greens such as endives and cabbages, whose robust flavors fortify us as the days and nights grow colder, are cut from sturdy stalks.

Autumn's bounty welcomes us into the warmth of the kitchen, there to transform the season's harvest into our favorite cold-weather dishes. Deep pots, porcelain baking dishes and heavy roasting pans are pulled from the cupboard to boil up steaming soups and stews or to hold golden-brown birds and bubbling, fruit-laden desserts. For the first time in months, entertaining also comes indoors, where meals are enhanced by the flicker of candles and firelight in the growing absence of the sun.

Selecting Autumn Ingredients

Autumn Vegetables. The autumn harvest brings us a wonderfully diverse selection of vegetables whose very variety calls for discerning senses. When selecting hard-shelled **winter squashes,** opt for those specimens that are heavy for their size and have a good overall color; reject any that are cracked or have soft spots that indicate decay. Look for **pumpkins** marked with tiny brown dots on their skin, a sign of sweetness. **Mushrooms** should appear firm and plump and feel slightly spongy to the touch; their skins should be neither very dry nor overly moist, and they should have a fresh, clean, earthy scent.

Autumn's cooling temperatures bring out a sweetness in **parsnips** and **rutabagas** (swedes), of which smaller specimens will have a finer flavor and texture. Select those that feel firm and heavy for their size and are blemish free. The same buying guidelines hold true for **potatoes and sweet potatoes,** with the added advice to choose those with skins in good condition and fairly free of eyes and, in the case of potatoes, any green spots.

Members of the **chicory family,** specifically escarole (Batavian endive), Belgian endive (chicory/witloof) and frisée, will have the best flavor and texture if harvested on the young side; lighter, more central leaves will have a milder taste and more tender texture. **Cabbages** should be heavy for their size, and their leaves should look crisp and fresh and be free of any streaks or other blemishes; the red variety, furthermore, should not show any hint of black along its edges. The same general rules apply to **Brussels sprouts.** The heads of **broccoli** and **cauliflower** should be compact, with no signs of blossoming or otherwise opening up, and their stalks should be uniformly firm.

Like other members of the onion family, **shallots** and **pearl onions** should have dry skins and feel firm. The bulb ends of **leeks** and **bulb fennel** are ideally crisp and white, and their leaves should appear healthy and green with no signs of wilting.

Although vegetable fruits are primarily a treat of summer, some remain in peak season into autumn. At their best, **eggplants** (aubergines) and **red bell peppers** (capsicums) are firm and have bright, glossy, unmarred skins. Most garden **herbs** will continue to flourish from the summer months well into the autumn season; transfer more delicate herbs to pots and place them indoors on sunny windowsills when the weather turns cold.

Like most autumn fruit, underripe pears reach maturity in a few days at room temperature.

Autumn Fruits. The fruits of autumn are, for the most part, on the hardy side, and it is easy to find them in good condition. **Pears,** for example, are generally picked and sold while still unripe and very firm. Avoid buying any that appear heavily bruised or have soft spots on either end. To ripen them, store at room temperature until they give to gentle finger pressure. Look for **apples** that are firm to the touch, a sign of crispness, and are free of bruises. The same attributes also indicate good **quinces,** which are green when unripe and uniformly pale yellow and sweetly scented when ripened at room temperature. **Figs** with slightly cracked skins are especially juicy and sweet; use them soon after purchase. Size, as well as a shiny skin, is a plus for **pomegranates,** with the largest having the juiciest kernels. Smooth skins, bright color and intact green caps indicate **persimmons** in good condition. The Hachiya variety must be soft before using; freeze hard Hachiyas for at least 24 hours, then thaw to ripen them quickly. The Fuyu variety is eaten while still firm. **Grapes** of all varieties should be plump and shiny.

Ripe persimmons still hang on the tree long after the leaves have fallen.

Autumn Fruits

Pears

1. Seckel
Comparatively small variety with thick, russet-yellow skin, buttery yet firm flesh and spicy flavor. Available from late summer through mid-winter. Good for eating plain, poaching and preserving.

2. French Butter
Plump, yellow-green fruit with a smooth, rich, butterlike texture and a delicate flavor accented by a hint of lemony acidity. Available from midsummer to early autumn. Good for eating raw or cooking.

3. Bartlett
Medium-sized, bell-shaped, early autumn pears with pale green to golden, and sometimes red, skin. Creamy-textured, mild, sweet and juicy flesh has a sweet, distinctive fragrance. Available from early summer to early November. Equally good for eating, cooking and preserving. Also called Williams' pears.

4. Bosc
Medium-sized to large, slender, tapered pears with yellow, green and russet skins, buttery yet spicy flavor and firm, slightly grainy flesh. Available from late summer to early spring. Good for eating or for cooking by any method.

5. Comice
Large, round pears with short necks, red-tinged, speckled greenish yellow skins and soft, juicy, aromatic flesh. Usually enjoyed raw. Available from midsummer through late autumn.

6. Anjou
Large, plump pears with short necks and thin, often russet-yellow skins. Available from autumn to early winter. Medium-grained to coarse-textured and juicy, with a hint of spice. Popular for cooking when slightly underripe, or for eating raw when fully ripened. Also sold as d'Anjou.

Apples

7. Pippin
Firm, crisp apples with green to yellow-green skin and a slightly tart, refreshing flavor. Well suited to eating raw on its own or using in fruit salads or baked desserts.

8. Rome Beauty
Bright red apples, sometimes striped with yellow, enjoyed for their juiciness and slightly tart flavor. Available throughout autumn and into late spring. The apple of choice for baking, in part because it holds its round shape so well; it may also be eaten raw.

9. Red Delicious
Big, sweet-tart, crisp and juicy apples with distinctive bright red skins. Best suited to eating raw on its own or in fruit salads.

10. Granny Smith
Native to Australia and notable for their bright green skins, these crisp, juicy apples are refresh-

13. Mission Figs
California variety of a fruit mentioned often in the Bible. Prized for its soft, dark purple-black skin and sweet pink flesh, which may be enjoyed eaten raw, baked in desserts or preserved. Also called Black Mission.

14. Pomegranates
Sometimes known as Chinese apples, these large, spherical, heavy fruits are first distinguished by their skins, ranging in color from yellow-orange to red to deep purple. Beneath the skin, embedded in spongy white membranes, is an abundance of tightly packed seeds (according to Persian folklore, precisely 613), each enclosed in juicy ruby-red flesh. For easy peeling, the pomegranate's skin is scored with a sharp knife and the bitter white membrane surrounding the kernels is discarded (see technique, page 15). The seeds may be enjoyed on their own or used as an edible garnish for fruit desserts or salads. More often, however, their juice—which stains easily—is extracted for use as a flavoring, sometimes sweetened and boiled down to make a syrup. Commercial grenadine syrup is derived from pomegranate juice.

15. Persimmons
Native to Asia, these autumn fruits are enjoyed for their bright orange color, lustrous, smooth skins and the delectable tart-sweet character of their orange flesh. Tomato-shaped Fuyu persimmons (shown here) are best enjoyed while still as crisp as an apple, although they eventually soften. More widely available heart-shaped Hachiya persimmons must be ripened to a point of complete, mushy softness; before that time, the fruit tastes unpleasantly astringent.

Grapes

16. Ruby
Very sweet and juicy seedless grapes with distinctive purplish red, tender skins and a pleasantly firm, crisp texture. Flame Seedless and Ribier are similar varieties.

17. Thompson Seedless
Widely available California-grown variety of medium-sized, slightly elongated grapes with pale green skins and mild, sweet, refreshingly juicy flesh.

ingly tart. They are often enjoyed raw. They are also a good choice for cooking because they hold their shape well.

11. McIntosh
Slightly tart, juicy and tender apple, Canadian in origin, with distinctive red-and-green skin. Available from late summer to late spring, but at the height of their season in autumn. Excellent for eating or for use in applesauce and baked desserts.

Other Tree Fruits

12. Quinces
Ancient fruits of central Asia that look like large, slightly lumpy apples or pears. Unpleasantly hard and rough-textured when raw, the fruits soften during cooking, acquiring a lovely pink cast in the process. High in pectin, quinces are frequently made into jams or jellies. They should be skinned and cored before cooking, and their raw flesh must be rubbed with lemon juice to prevent discoloration.

Autumn Vegetables

Winter Squashes

1. Acorn Squashes
Acorn-shaped medium-sized squashes, up to 8 inches (20 cm) long, with ribbed, dark green skin that turns orange with storage. The mild, sweet flavor and light, smooth texture of the orange flesh is best complemented by baking.

2. Turban Squashes
Squashes with flattened, circular, bumpy orange bases up to 15 inches (37.5 cm) in diameter crowned by distinctive, smaller turban-shaped orange tops with blue-green stripes. The flesh is bright orange and rich in flavor.

3. Butternut Squash
Cylindrical squashes up to 12 inches (30 cm) in length, with the flower end slightly enlarged to a bulblike shape. The flesh is bright orange, moist and fairly sweet.

4. Spaghetti Squashes
Until recently grown largely in home gardens as a novelty vegetable, this elongated, melon-shaped, yellow-skinned squash takes its name from the long, thin strands into which its flesh separates after cooking. It has a mild flavor and delicately crunchy texture. Now commercially grown in California and Florida.

5. Sugar Pumpkins
Smaller, globe-shaped relatives of the familiar pumpkin, with bright orange, ridged skin and deep orange, dense, and very sweet flesh.

6. Hubbard Squashes
Large, irregularly shaped squashes with an often unattractive, greenish gray shell concealing rich orange flesh.

Mushrooms

7. Porcini
The common Italian term for *Boletus edulis* and also known by the French name *cèpes*. Porcini grow wild throughout North America and may be found from middle to late fall. Very plump,

which explains their Italian name of "little pigs," these popular brown-capped, thick-stemmed mushrooms have a rich, meaty flavor with hints of hazelnut (filbert). They are best appreciated by grilling or baking, but may also be eaten raw and thinly sliced.

8. Shiitakes
Rich and meaty, this Asian variety, once harvested in the wild, is now cultivated commercially. The caps are notable for their velvety dark brown color and their flat, floppy, cir-cular shape. The stems, which are quite tough, must be trimmed away before cooking.

9. Button Mushrooms
Immature variety of common cultivated mushrooms harvested soon after they have first emerged from the soil, when their caps are still small and tightly closed, resembling buttons. Good eaten raw, in salads, or lightly cooked to preserve their delicate texture and flavor. Select those with gills fully concealed. Also known as common white mushrooms.

cooked in the oven rather than boiled when intended for mashing.

12. Parsnips

Although similar in shape and texture to the carrot, this ivory-colored root, which first appears in abundance in markets around mid-autumn, is never eaten raw. Cooked, however, it has an appealingly sweet, rich, almost nutlike flavor. Although the Italians feed parsnips to the pigs they raise for their famed Parma hams, Americans have prized parsnips as a popular staple since early colonial days, when they were mistakenly believed to be poisonous if pulled before the first frost. Deep, cold storage does, however, sweeten their flavor, transforming the root's starch into sugar.

13. Rutabagas

Also known as swedes or Swedish turnips. Although these spherical, ivory-and-purple–skinned roots resemble large turnips, they are members of the cabbage family, with their own distinctively sweet, pale yellow-orange flesh. Rutabagas were introduced to America from Europe by Thomas Jefferson.

14. Rose Fir Potatoes

Small to medium-sized waxy potatoes with thin, delicate, pale pink skins and creamy, flavorful flesh.

15. Red Potatoes

Various types of small to medium-sized potatoes with red skins and creamy flesh that, depending on the variety, may range in color from ivory to pale red. Generally good for boiling.

16. Yukon Gold Potatoes

Small to medium-sized, waxy-fleshed potatoes, available in markets only in recent years. Prized for their golden color, rich, buttery flavor and creamy texture. Ideal for baking, panfrying, mashing and gratins.

17. Purple Potatoes

Small to medium-sized potatoes with tender purple skins and flavorful white or purple flesh; suitable for boiling, mashing or frying.

18. Yellow Finn Potatoes

Similar in texture and flavor to the Yukon Gold (see above); well suited to roasting, frying, baking or mashing.

10. Chanterelles

Distinguished by their pale gold color that is sometimes compared to that of scrambled eggs and by their 2–3-inch (5–7.5-cm) trumpetlike shapes, these woodland mushrooms are prized for fine flavor that can range from nutlike to meaty. Available throughout the autumn months, they are now also cultivated commercially in the Pacific Northwest. Before use, brush away any dirt with a mushroom brush or paper towel; do not rinse or the mushrooms will become soggy.

Roots and Tubers

11. Sweet Potatoes

Not true potatoes, although resembling them in form, these tubers from a tropical American plant have light tan to deep red skins and pale yellow to orange flesh prized for its sweetness. The light-skinned variety is the most common. Sweet potatoes may be cooked in any of the ways common for regular potatoes; baking, however, tends to intensify their natural sweetness, so sweet potatoes are often

Autumn Vegetables and Herbs

Chicory Family

1. Escarole
Also known as Batavian endive. Variety of chicory with broad, bright green, refreshingly bitter leaves.

2. Belgian Endive
Crisp, white, spear-shaped leaves edged with pale yellow-green or pinkish red, tightly packed in small, cone-shaped heads. The slight bitterness, mildest in smaller heads, comes through both raw and cooked. Also known as chicory or witloof.

3. Frisée
Head of frilly leaves with a bitter edge of flavor that is at its mildest at the paler center.

Bulbs

4. Leeks
Long, cylindrical members of the onion family with white root ends, dark green leaves and a delicate, sweet flavor that has earned them the nickname of "poor man's asparagus." All leeks are grown in sandy soil and require thorough washing with cold running water to remove any grit lodged between their multi-layered leaves. Leeks enjoy a long season; look for them in markets from late summer to early spring.

5. Fennel
Autumn sees the year's second crop of this plant related to the herb of the same name; the first comes in spring. Its bulbous cluster of stalk bases has a crisp, celerylike texture and a mild, sweet anise flavor.

6. Shallots
These smaller relatives of the onion are thought by some to resemble in taste a cross between onion and garlic, making them a popular seasoning in their own right.

7. Pearl Onions
These immature onions of many varieties are picked in summer when small and dried for use in autumn. Flavor tends to be fairly pungent, but cooking or preserving brings out a rich sweetness. Pearl onions must be peeled before eating. A special technique removes the skin and keeps the layers intact during cooking (see technique, page 15).

Brassicas

8. Napa Cabbage
Also known as Chinese cabbage or celery cabbage, the latter for the juicy crispness of its long, mild, pale green to white leaves. Available in Asian markets and well-stocked food stores.

9. Red Cabbage
At the peak of its almost 10-month-long season in autumn, this variety has crisp, tightly packed leaves ranging from dark purplish red to bright crimson.

10. Green Cabbage
Firm cabbage with fairly smooth, pale green leaves tightly packed in a compact sphere.

11. Savoy Cabbage
Firm, round, fine-flavored variety of cabbage with dark green leaves marked by a lacy pattern of pale green veins.

12. Broccoli
Cabbage family member with green to purple-green, tightly clustered, unopened budding sprouts—known as florets—growing at the end of sturdy stalks. Both the florets and the stems, if the latter are thickly peeled, may be eaten. Although available year-round, broccoli prefers

available to Western cooks, still abundantly available in autumn, is the large, plump globe eggplant shown here; long, slender Asian eggplants, which have fewer seeds and are considered finer in flavor and texture, may also be found during this season.

16. Red Bell Peppers

Crisp-fleshed, bell-shaped peppers (capsicums) have a mild flavor that grows ever sweeter as they mature in autumn from green to their fully ripened red state. Whether enjoyed raw or roasted, peppers should have their stems and white interior ribs cut or pulled out and their seeds removed before use.

Fresh Herbs

17. Rosemary

Mediterranean herb, used either fresh or dried. The needlelike leaves, sometimes decked in tiny blue flowers, have a highly aromatic flavor well suited to lamb, veal, pork, poultry, seafood and vegetables. Use sparingly, as the strong taste can overpower dishes.

18. Parsley

A native of southern Europe, this widely popular fresh herb is available in two main types: the more common curly-leaf parsley, a popular garnish, and flat-leaf parsley (shown here), also known as Italian parsley, which has a more pronounced flavor and is preferred for seasoning.

19. Thyme

An ancient eastern Mediterranean herb prized for its fragrant, clean-tasting small leaves that complement poultry, light meats, seafood or vegetables. Also commonly available in a lemon-scented variety.

20. Sage

Strong flavored herb, used either fresh or dried in the cuisines of Europe and the Middle East. Well suited to fresh or cured pork, lamb, veal or poultry, as well as some sauces and salads.

21. Bay Leaves

Pungent, spicy dried whole leaves of the bay laurel tree, which grows abundantly in the Mediterranean and in similar sunny climates such as that of California. Commonly used as a seasoning in simmered dishes, including soups and braises or stews of meat or seafood; in marinades for those same main ingredients; and in pickling mixtures. French bay leaves, sometimes found in specialty-food shops, possess a milder, sweeter flavor than those from California.

cool growing conditions and is at its best during the autumn months.

13. Cauliflower

Member of the cabbage family bred for its tightly clustered, ivory (bottom) or sometimes purple (top), unopened budding heads. Both the heads, which may be separated into florets, and the more tender parts of the stems may be eaten. The vegetable grows especially well in autumn's cool climate.

14. Brussels Sprouts

A species of cabbage first selectively bred in Belgium in the 13th century to form bite-sized, perfect little balls clustered on a heavy stalk.

They develop their best flavor under autumn's cool growing conditions. Brussels sprouts are sometimes found in farmers' markets still on their stalk, although they are more commonly sold already detached.

Vegetable Fruits

15. Eggplants

Of Asian origin, the eggplant (aubergine) migrated across the Middle East to Europe, reaching Italy by the 15th century. Its multitude of varieties include many different shapes and sizes, among them an ivory-skinned one resembling a goose egg, the source of its English name. The most common variety

Autumn Techniques

IN AUTUMN, nature seems to toughen us up for the approaching rigors of winter by making us work a little harder to enjoy her seasonal bounty. Hard-shelled squashes must be halved and cooked before their tender flesh can be savored. The leathery skins of pomegranates and the shells of chestnuts are methodically stripped away to reveal the treasures concealed within. Even something as seemingly uncomplicated as a pearl onion requires a quick peeling techique to conserve its outermost layers of flesh and to keep it intact while it cooks.

The quintessential autumn main course, a whole roast turkey, also demands a little extra work—in this case careful trussing, basting and carving so that it can be served and enjoyed at its festive best.

Roasting a Turkey

A turkey is trussed before roasting to give it a compact shape that cooks more evenly and looks more attractive. Diligent basting during roasting yields moist results.

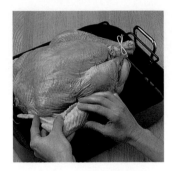

Stuff the turkey. Tie the drumsticks together with kitchen string. Place the turkey, breast side up, on a rack in a roasting pan. Secure the wings against the bird by tucking their tips beneath the breast (left).

Roast the turkey at 400°F (200°C) for 45 minutes, then drape it with butter-soaked cheesecloth (muslin). Continue roasting at 325°F (165°C), basting every 30 minutes, until the turkey tests done.

Carving a Turkey

Before carving, let the turkey rest at room temperature for 20 minutes, tenting it with aluminum foil to keep it warm. Hot juices will settle back into the meat, yielding moister meat that cuts more smoothly.

Place the turkey on a carving board. Pull back the leg to locate the thigh joint; cut through it with a sharp knife to remove. Cut apart the thigh and drumstick. Carve the breasts into thin slices.

Winter Squash Techniques

The firm flesh of hard winter squashes becomes tender and sweet when baked, boiled or steamed. Once cooked, the flesh can then be easily scooped out or, for spaghetti squash, removed in long, thin strands.

Cut the squash—here, acorn squash—in half. Bake, cut sides down, on a baking sheet. Let cool. With a spoon, scoop out the seeds and fiber, discarding them, and then spoon out the tender flesh.

Once a spaghetti squash has been cooked, let cool, then cut in half and scoop out and discard the seeds. Using a fork, gently scrape out the flesh, which will separate into spaghettilike strands.

Seeding Pomegranates

Using the correct technique, seeding pomegranates can be easy and free of any juicy mess. Simply score the skin with a knife and pull the seeds away in a bowl of water.

Score the pomegranate skin into quarters. Submerge the fruit in a bowl of water and peel away the skin. Then pull the seeds from the membrane, letting them sink to the bottom of the bowl.

Peeling Pearl Onions

Pearl onions are appealing because each one can be eaten in a single bite. This peeling technique not only removes their skins easily with minimal waste but also helps keep the onions' layers from separating during cooking.

Boil the onions in water for 2 minutes. Drain, rinse with cold water and drain again. Trim the root ends, then cut a shallow X on the trimmed end to prevent the layers from telescoping during cooking.

One at a time, grasp each trimmed onion between your thumb and fingertips. Squeeze gently but firmly to pop the onion from its outermost layer of skin.

Peeling Chestnuts

A specialty of autumn, fresh chestnuts have tough, brown outer shells and fuzzy inner coats that must be removed before the nuts can be eaten.

Cut a shallow X on the flat side of each chestnut. Cook in simmering water until the nut meats are tender when pierced, 45–55 minutes. Drain, then peel away the hard shells and inner sheaths.

Autumn Basics

Corn Bread

Delicious freshly baked or dried for use in stuffings *(see page 66)*.

1½ cups (7½ oz/235 g) all-purpose (plain) flour

1½ cups (7½ oz/235 g) cornmeal

2 tablespoons sugar

1 tablespoon baking powder

1 teaspoon salt

1 cup (8 fl oz/250 ml) milk

1 cup (8 fl oz/250 ml) sour cream

⅓ cup (3 fl oz/80 ml) corn oil

1 egg, lightly beaten

PREHEAT AN OVEN to 375°F (190°C). Butter a 9-inch (23-cm) square cake pan.

Sift together the flour, cornmeal, sugar, baking powder and salt into a bowl. In another bowl, whisk the milk, sour cream, corn oil and egg. Fold into the flour mixture; do not overmix. Pour into the prepared pan.

Bake until a toothpick inserted into the center comes out clean, about 35 minutes. Remove from the oven and let stand for 10 minutes, then turn out onto a rack to cool. Cut into squares. *Makes one 9-inch (23-cm) square loaf; serves 9*

Smoked Cheddar Twists

Perfect for serving with wine or aperitifs, these crisp twists can also be made with aged Cheddar or pepper Jack in place of the smoked Cheddar.

1 cup (5 oz/155 g) all-purpose (plain) flour

⅓ cup (1½ oz/45 g) cake (soft-wheat) flour

¼ teaspoon cayenne pepper

½ cup (2 oz/60 g) shredded smoked Cheddar cheese

¼ cup (1 oz/30 g) grated Parmesan cheese

¼ teaspoon salt

¾ cup (6 oz/185 g) unsalted butter, cut into pieces

2 teaspoons fresh lemon juice

¼ cup (2 fl oz/60 ml) ice water

IN THE WORK BOWL of a food processor fitted with the metal blade, combine the all-purpose flour, cake flour, cayenne pepper, Cheddar cheese, Parmesan cheese and salt. Pulse to mix. Sprinkle the butter pieces over the flour mixture and place the work bowl in the freezer for 1 hour, then pulse again to combine.

In a small bowl, mix the lemon juice and ice water. With the processor on, add just enough of the lemon juice mixture to the flour mixture for it to come together in a rough mass.

Turn out the dough onto a lightly floured board and gently form into a rough rectangle; do not overwork. Using a rolling pin, roll out into a rectangle ½ inch (12 mm) thick. Fold in the narrow ends to meet in the center. Then fold in half crosswise so that there are 4 layers. Turn the dough a quarter turn and roll out again to form a rectangle ½ inch (12 mm) thick. Fold the rectangle into thirds as if you are folding a letter. Wrap the dough in plastic wrap and refrigerate for 45 minutes.

Preheat an oven to 400°F (200°C). Unwrap the dough and place on a floured work surface. Roll out into a rectangle about 7 inches (18 cm) wide by 15 inches (38 cm) long by ⅛ inch (3 mm) thick. Trim the edges so that they are even. Cut the dough crosswise into sticks ½ inch (12 mm) wide and twist each one once to form a soft turn at the center. Place the twists on 2 ungreased baking sheets, spacing them about 1 inch (2.5 cm) apart.

Bake until golden and crisp, about 15 minutes, switching the baking sheets about halfway through baking. Let cool. Serve immediately, or pack into an airtight container and store at room temperature for up to 1 week. *Makes about 30 twists*

GLAZED SPICED NUTS

Eaten as they are or sprinkled on salads or desserts, these nuts make a simple yet festive addition to the autumn table.

¾ cup (4 oz/125 g) blanched whole almonds

¾ cup (3 oz/90 g) pecan halves

¾ cup (3 oz/90 g) walnut halves

1 egg white

¼ cup (2 oz/60 g) sugar

2 teaspoons grated orange zest

1 teaspoon salt

1 teaspoon ground cumin

½ teaspoon freshly ground pepper

½ teaspoon red pepper flakes

PREHEAT AN OVEN to 375°F (190°C).

Spread the nuts on a baking sheet and toast until lightly golden and fragrant, 5–7 minutes. Let cool. Reduce the oven temperature to 325°F (165°C).

In a bowl, beat the egg white until frothy. Add the nuts and toss to coat evenly.

In another bowl, mix the sugar, orange zest, salt, cumin, pepper and red pepper flakes. Add the nuts, toss to coat and spread in a single layer on the baking sheet.

Bake until golden, 20–25 minutes. Let cool completely before serving. Store in an airtight container at room temperature for up to 2 weeks. *Makes 2¼ cups (10 oz/315 g)*

PEAR AND APPLESAUCE

Comice or Bartlett (Williams') pears are an excellent choice for making this sauce. Gravenstein, McIntosh, Granny Smith or pippins are suitable apple varieties. Serve as an accompaniment to autumn's hearty roasts and stews.

1½ lb (750 g) pears *(see note)*

1½ lb (750 g) apples *(see note)*

¼ cup (2 fl oz/60 ml) water, or as needed

5 tablespoons (4 oz/125 g) honey

2 tablespoons fresh lemon juice

½ teaspoon ground cinnamon

¼ teaspoon ground nutmeg

⅛ teaspoon ground cloves

1 tablespoon pear brandy or brandy

PEEL THE PEARS AND APPLES, then halve, core and cut into ½-inch (12-mm) pieces.

In a saucepan, combine the pears, apples, ¼ cup (2 fl oz/60 ml) water, and the honey, lemon juice, cinnamon, nutmeg and cloves. Stir well and place over medium heat. Bring to a simmer and cook uncovered, stirring occasionally, until the pears and apples are soft but retain their shape and the liquid is absorbed, about 30 minutes. If the mixture begins to dry out, add more water as needed.

Stir in the pear brandy. Serve warm or at room temperature. *Makes about 3 cups (1¾ lb/875 g)*

CRANBERRY AND ZINFANDEL RELISH

When the British colonists arrived in America, cranberries were already a staple of the Native Americans. Since then, the berries have come to symbolize autumn and the holiday table. The berries are cultivated in sandy bogs, where they are harvested from low-lying vines.

2½ cups (20 fl oz/625 ml) red Zinfandel wine

¾ cup (6 oz/185 g) sugar

5 orange peel strips, each 2 inches (5 cm) long

4 cinnamon sticks

10 whole cloves

3 cups (12 fl oz/375 g) cranberries

IN A SAUCEPAN over high heat, combine the wine, sugar, orange peel, cinnamon sticks and cloves. Bring to a boil, stirring to dissolve the sugar. Reduce the heat to medium and simmer, stirring occasionally, until the liquid thickens slightly, about 15 minutes. Strain and return the liquid to the pan.

Add the cranberries and raise the heat to high. Boil until the berries pop, 5–10 minutes. Reduce the heat to low and simmer until the mixture thickens slightly, 20–30 minutes. Transfer to a bowl and let cool before serving. *Makes about 2 cups (1¼ lb/625 g)*

openers

...and you whose pastime
Is to make midnight mushrooms, that rejoice
To hear the solemn curfew.

—William Shakespeare

Mushroom and Stilton Galette

For the pastry:

1¼ cups (6½ oz/200 g) all-purpose (plain) flour

¼ teaspoon salt

½ cup (4 oz/125 g) unsalted butter, cut into pieces

¼ cup (2 fl oz/60 ml) sour cream

2 teaspoons fresh lemon juice

¼ cup (2 fl oz/60 ml) ice water

For the filling:

¼ oz (7 g) dried wild mushrooms such as chanterelles, porcini or shiitakes

1 cup (8 fl oz/250 ml) boiling water

2 tablespoons unsalted butter

¾ cup (2 oz/60 g) sliced green (spring) onions

1 clove garlic, minced

½ teaspoon chopped fresh rosemary

½ teaspoon chopped fresh thyme

½ lb (250 g) assorted fresh wild mushrooms such as chanterelles, porcini and shiitakes, brushed clean and large mushrooms thinly sliced

½ lb (250 g) fresh button mushrooms, brushed clean and thinly sliced

5 oz (155 g) Stilton or other good-quality blue cheese

During the damp autumn months, professional mushroom foragers and amateurs alike seek out prized fungi in fields and forests.

TO MAKE THE PASTRY, combine the flour and salt in a bowl. Place the butter in another bowl. Place both bowls in the freezer for 1 hour. Remove the bowls from the freezer and make a well in the center of the flour. Add the butter to the well and, using a pastry blender, cut it in until the mixture has the consistency of coarse meal. Make another well in the center. In a small bowl, whisk together the sour cream, lemon juice and water and add half of this mixture to the well. With your fingertips, mix in the liquid until large lumps form. Remove the large lumps and repeat with the remaining liquid and flour-butter mixture. Pat the lumps into a ball; do not overwork the dough. Wrap in plastic wrap and refrigerate for 1 hour.

Meanwhile, make the filling: Place the dried mushrooms in a small bowl and add the boiling water. Let stand for 30 minutes until softened. Drain the mushrooms and mince finely. Preheat an oven to 400°F (200°C).

In a large frying pan over medium heat, melt the butter. Add the green onions and sauté, stirring occasionally, until soft, about 5 minutes. Add the garlic, rosemary and thyme and continue to cook, stirring, for 1 minute longer. Raise the heat to high, add the fresh and rehydrated mushrooms and sauté until the mushrooms are tender and the liquid they released has completely evaporated, 8–10 minutes. Transfer to a plate and let cool.

On a floured work surface, roll out the dough into a 12-inch (30-cm) round. Transfer to an ungreased baking sheet. Crumble the blue cheese into a bowl, add the cooled mushrooms and stir well. Spread the mixture over the dough, leaving a 1½-inch (4-cm) border. Fold the border over the mushrooms and cheese, pleating the edge to make it fit. The center will be open.

Bake until golden brown, 30–40 minutes. Remove from the oven, let stand for 5 minutes, then slide the galette onto a serving plate. Serve hot, warm or at room temperature, cut into wedges. *Serves 6*

Grilled Bread with Fresh Shell Beans and Escarole

1	**lb (500 g) fresh shell beans** *(see note)*
3	**cloves garlic, minced**
2	**tablespoons chopped fresh sage**
3	**tablespoons extra-virgin olive oil, plus olive oil for brushing**
	salt and freshly ground pepper
18	**slices country-style bread, about 3 inches (7.5 cm) in diameter**
½	**head escarole (Batavian endive), cored and cut into strips 1 inch (2.5 cm) wide**
1	**tablespoon red wine vinegar**
	small pinch of red pepper flakes

Although fresh shell beans can be found in markets during July and August, the abundance and variety increase during late summer and into the autumn months. The palette is enormous, from American varieties such as cranberry, pinto and lima to Italian borlotti and cannellini and French flageolets. Each pod contains three or four beans. They take a bit of work to shell but are well worth the effort.

SHELL THE BEANS. Bring a saucepan three-fourths full of water to a boil over medium-high heat. Add the beans and cook until very soft, about 20 minutes. Drain, reserving 1 cup (8 fl oz/250 ml) of the liquid.

Prepare a fire in a charcoal grill or preheat a broiler (griller). In a frying pan over medium heat, combine the beans, garlic, sage, and 2 tablespoons of the oil. Cook, mashing the beans with a spoon or potato masher and adding the reserved cooking liquid as needed to keep the mixture moist, until a rough paste forms, 10–15 minutes. Remove from the heat and continue mashing the beans to form a smooth paste. Alternatively, pulse the mixture in a food processor fitted with the metal blade or in a blender. Season to taste with salt and pepper.

Lightly brush the bread slices on both sides with olive oil and place on the grill rack or on a baking sheet. Grill or broil, turning once, until golden on both sides, 30–60 seconds on each side. Remove from the heat and set aside.

In another frying pan over high heat, warm the remaining 1 tablespoon oil. Add the escarole and cook, tossing frequently with tongs, until wilted, 2–3 minutes. Add the vinegar and red pepper flakes and season to taste with salt and pepper. Mix well.

To serve, spread the bean purée on the grilled or toasted bread, dividing it evenly. Top with the wilted escarole and serve immediately. *Makes 18 pieces; serves 6*

Sweet Potato Soufflé

2	lb (1 kg) sweet potatoes
½	cup (2 oz/60 g) freshly grated Parmesan cheese
3	tablespoons unsalted butter
1	white onion, minced
1½	cups (12 fl oz/375 ml) milk
3	tablespoons all-purpose (plain) flour
¼	teaspoon freshly grated nutmeg
¼	teaspoon ground allspice
¼	teaspoon ground ginger
6	eggs, separated
1	cup (4 oz/125 g) shredded Gruyère cheese
	salt and freshly ground pepper

Contrary to popular belief, the tuberous roots most people refer to as sweet potatoes or yams are not related to the russet potato. These natives of the New World are members of the morning glory family. Their characteristic sweetness develops even further after harvest.

PREHEAT AN OVEN to 375°F (190°C).

Pierce the potatoes two or three times with a fork and place on a baking sheet. Bake until easily pierced with a knife, 30–40 minutes. Remove from the oven and let cool. Cut in half and scrape out the pulp into a bowl. Using a potato masher, mash to form a smooth purée; you should have 2½ cups (1¼ lb/625 g). Leave the oven temperature set at 375°F (190°C).

Butter a 2-qt (2-l) soufflé dish and dust the bottom and sides with ¼ cup (1 oz/30 g) of the Parmesan cheese.

In a large saucepan over medium heat, melt the butter. Add the onion and sauté, stirring occasionally, until soft, about 10 minutes. Meanwhile, in a small saucepan over medium heat, warm the milk until small bubbles appear along the edges of the pan; remove from the heat. Add the flour to the onion and cook, stirring constantly, for 3 minutes. (Do not brown.) Whisk in the milk all at once and simmer, continuing to whisk, until thickened, 2–3 minutes. Remove from the heat and stir in the nutmeg, allspice and ginger. Add the egg yolks one at a time, beating well after each addition. Add the sweet potato purée and the Gruyère cheese and stir until well blended. Season to taste with salt and pepper.

In a bowl, using an electric mixer set on high speed, beat the egg whites until they just hold stiff peaks. Using a rubber spatula, fold one-fourth of the egg whites into the sweet potato mixture to lighten it. Then gently fold in the remaining whites just until no white streaks remain. Pour into the prepared soufflé dish. Sprinkle with the remaining ¼ cup (1 oz/30 g) Parmesan cheese.

Bake until puffed and golden, 45–50 minutes. Serve immediately. *Serves 6*

Crown'd with the sickle, and the wheaten sheaf,
While Autumn, nodding o'er the yellow plain,
Comes jovial on.

—James Thomson

Focaccia with Grapes and Walnuts

¼   **cup (2 fl oz/60 ml) extra-virgin olive oil, plus olive oil for brushing**

3   **fresh rosemary sprigs**

½   **cup (2 oz/60 g) walnuts, very coarsely chopped**

2   **cups (10 oz/315 g) all-purpose (plain) flour, plus flour for kneading**

1   **tablespoon active dry yeast**

¾   **cup (6 fl oz/180 ml) luke-warm water (110°F/43°C)**

1   **tablespoon aniseeds, coarsely ground in a mortar or spice grinder**

1½   **teaspoons coarse salt**

2   **tablespoons sugar**

1½   **cups (9 oz/280 g) grapes, one variety or a mixture**

The word *focaccia* comes from the Italian word *focolare,* meaning "hearth," which is where these dimpled Tuscan breads were traditionally cooked.

IN A FRYING PAN or saucepan over medium heat, warm the ¼ cup (2 fl oz/ 60 ml) olive oil and rosemary until they sizzle, about 2 minutes. Remove from the heat, add the walnuts and let cool. Discard the rosemary sprigs.

In a small bowl, stir together ¼ cup (1½ oz/45 g) of the flour, the yeast and ¼ cup (2 fl oz/60 ml) of the lukewarm water. Let stand until bubbles form on the surface, about 20 minutes. Add the aniseeds, ½ teaspoon of the salt, the sugar, the remaining ½ cup (4 fl oz/120 ml) lukewarm water, and the walnuts and rosemary oil. Using a wooden spoon, stir in the remaining 1¾ cups (8½ oz/270 g) flour. Turn out onto a floured work surface and knead until smooth and elastic, about 10 minutes, adding just enough flour as needed to prevent sticking. Place in a well-oiled bowl and turn the dough to oil the top. Cover the bowl with plastic wrap and let the dough rise in a warm place until doubled in volume, about 1 hour.

Position a rack in the bottom third of an oven and place a pizza stone on the rack. Preheat the oven to 450°F (230°C).

Punch down the dough and turn out onto a well-floured work surface. Using a rolling pin, roll out into an 8-by-10-inch (20-by-25-cm) oval about ½ inch (12 mm) thick. Transfer the oval to a well-floured pizza peel or a rimless baking sheet. Using your fingertips, make shallow indentations in the surface of the dough, spacing them about 1½ inches (4 cm) apart. Press the grapes into the indentations. Brush the surface of the round with olive oil. Sprinkle the remaining 1 teaspoon salt evenly over the surface. Slide the focaccia directly onto the stone. Bake until golden and crisp, 15–20 minutes. Serve hot, warm or at room temperature. *Serves 6*

Curried Pumpkin and Leek Flan

1 small pumpkin, 2 lb (1 kg) *(see note)*

2 tablespoons unsalted butter

6 leeks, including 1 inch (2.5 cm) of green, carefully rinsed and cut into ½-inch (12-mm) dice

3 whole eggs, plus 3 egg yolks

1½ cups (12 fl oz/375 ml) heavy (double) cream

2 tablespoons sugar

1 teaspoon curry powder

salt and freshly ground pepper

boiling water, as needed

1½ cups (12 fl oz/375 ml) chicken stock

1 tablespoon chopped fresh flat-leaf (Italian) parsley plus parsley sprigs for garnish

Sugar pumpkins are an excellent choice for baking and work well in this recipe. If unavailable, substitute any winter squash.

PREHEAT AN OVEN to 375°F (190°C). Lightly oil a baking sheet.

Cut the pumpkin in half through the stem end and place, cut side down, on the prepared baking sheet. Bake until easily pierced with a knife, 40–50 minutes. Remove from the oven and let cool. Leave the oven set at 375°F (190°C). Using a spoon, scoop out the seeds and fibers and discard. Spoon the flesh into a blender. Purée until smooth.

Meanwhile, in a large frying pan over medium heat, melt the butter. Add the leeks and cook, stirring occasionally, until they are very soft and begin to fall apart, 30–40 minutes. Remove from the heat.

In a bowl, whisk together the whole eggs and egg yolks, 1 cup (8 fl oz/250 ml) of the cream, the sugar, curry powder and salt and pepper to taste. Add three-fourths of the pumpkin purée and all the leeks and stir well.

Butter six ⅔-cup (5-fl oz/160-ml) ramekins or flan molds. Place in a large baking pan and divide the flan mixture evenly among the prepared molds. Pour boiling water into the baking pan to reach halfway up the sides of the molds. Cover the pan loosely with aluminum foil. Bake until the custards are firm in the center and browned on top, 20–25 minutes.

While the flans are baking, combine the chicken stock, the remaining pumpkin purée and the remaining ½ cup (4 fl oz/125 ml) cream in a saucepan. Place over medium-high heat and bring to a boil, stirring occasionally. Boil gently until reduced by half, 5–10 minutes. Strain through a fine-mesh sieve into a clean pan. Season to taste with salt and pepper.

Remove the flans from the oven and let cool for 5 minutes. Run a knife around the edge of each mold and invert onto individual plates. Ladle the sauce around the custards. Garnish with the parsley and serve. *Serves 6*

Fried Polenta Sticks with Sage

5   **cups (40 fl oz/1.1 l) water**

1   **teaspoon salt, plus salt to taste**

1¼   **cups (7½ oz/235 g) polenta**

½   **cup (2 oz/60 g) freshly grated Parmesan**

2   **tablespoons chopped fresh sage**

3   **tablespoons unsalted butter**

     freshly ground pepper

2   **cups (10 oz/315 g) all-purpose (plain) flour**

     olive oil and safflower oil for deep-frying

     fresh herb sprigs

The heartiness of polenta makes it a comforting menu addition when autumn's chill sets in. The coarse grains develop their characteristic mushiness while mixing them with simmering liquid, so reserve some stamina for stirring.

IN A HEAVY SAUCEPAN, bring the water to a boil over high heat and add the 1 teaspoon salt. Slowly add the polenta in a steady stream while whisking constantly. Continue to whisk until the mixture thickens, about 2 minutes. Switch to a wooden spoon, reduce the heat to medium and continue to simmer, stirring, until the polenta pulls away from the sides of the pan, 20–25 minutes. Add the Parmesan, sage and butter and stir to mix well. Season with salt and pepper to taste.

Butter a 9-inch (23-cm) square pan. Pour the hot polenta into the prepared pan and smooth the top with a rubber spatula. Let cool slightly, then cover and refrigerate until cold and set, at least 1 hour or for up to 3 days.

Using a sharp knife, cut the polenta into sticks 3 inches (7.5 cm) long by ½ inch (12 mm) wide. Toss them gently with the flour, dusting lightly.

Position a rack in the upper part of an oven and preheat to 400°F (200°C). Pour equal amounts of the olive and safflower oils into a large, deep frying pan to a depth of 2 inches (5 cm). Heat to 375°F (190°C) on a deep-frying thermometer. When hot, add the polenta sticks a few at a time and fry, turning occasionally with a slotted spoon or tongs, until golden brown, 1–2 minutes. Transfer to paper towels to drain, then keep warm in the oven until all are cooked.

Arrange the polenta sticks on a warmed platter and sprinkle with salt to taste. Garnish with herb sprigs and serve immediately. *Makes about 50 polenta sticks; serves 8*

Pizza with Winter Squash and Smoked Bacon

For the pizza dough:

¾ cup (6 fl oz/180 ml) luke-warm water (110°F/43°C)

2 teaspoons active dry yeast

2 cups (10 oz/315 g) all-purpose (plain) flour, plus flour as needed

3 tablespoons extra-virgin olive oil

½ teaspoon salt

For the pizza topping:

¼ small butternut squash, ½ lb (250 g), seeded, peeled and cut into thin slices

2 tablespoons extra-virgin olive oil

   salt and freshly ground pepper

¼ lb (125 g) hickory-smoked bacon, cut into small dice

3 oz (90 g) smoked mozzarella cheese, shredded

3 oz (90 g) plain mozzarella cheese, shredded

¼ cup (⅓ oz/10 g) chopped fresh sage

TO MAKE THE PIZZA DOUGH, in a bowl, stir together ¼ cup (2 fl oz/60 ml) of the water, the yeast and ¼ cup (1 oz/30 g) of the flour. Let stand until bubbly, about 20 minutes. Add the remaining ½ cup (4 fl oz/120 ml) lukewarm water, the olive oil and the salt. Stir in the remaining 1¾ cups (9 oz/285 g) flour and mix well. Turn out onto a floured work surface and knead until smooth and elastic, about 10 minutes. Place in a well-oiled bowl and turn the dough to oil the top. Cover the bowl with plastic wrap and let the dough rise in a warm place until doubled in volume, about 1 hour.

Position a rack in the bottom third of an oven and place a pizza stone on the rack. Preheat the oven to 500°F (260°C).

To make the topping, bring a saucepan three-fourths full of salted water to a boil. Add the squash slices and boil until half-cooked, about 3 minutes. Using a slotted spoon, transfer to paper towels and drain well. In a large frying pan over high heat, warm 1 tablespoon of the oil. Add the squash and cook, turning, until golden on the edges and cooked through, about 5 minutes. Season generously with salt and pepper. Remove the squash and let cool.

Add the remaining 1 tablespoon oil to the frying pan and place over medium heat. Add the bacon and cook, stirring, until it begins to turn golden, about 5 minutes. Using the slotted spoon, transfer to paper towels to drain. In a bowl, combine the mozzarella cheeses and toss to mix.

Punch down the dough and turn out onto a floured work surface. Divide in half and roll out one half into a round 9 inches (23 cm) in diameter and ¼ inch (6 mm) thick. Transfer to a well-floured pizza peel or rimless baking sheet. Sprinkle on half of the cheese, leaving a ½-inch (12-mm) border uncovered around the edges. Sprinkle with half each of the bacon and sage. Top with half of the squash slices. Slide the pizza directly onto the stone.

Bake until golden and crisp, 8–10 minutes. Repeat with the remaining ingredients. Serve at once. *Makes two 9-inch (23-cm) pizzas; serves 6*

soups
and salads

There is something in October
sets the gypsy blood astir.

—William Bliss Carmen

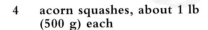

4   **acorn squashes, about 1 lb (500 g) each**

1   **tablespoon unsalted butter, at room temperature**

2   **slices bacon, 2 oz (60 g), finely chopped**

1   **large yellow onion, chopped**

6   **cups (48 fl oz/1.5 l) chicken stock**

For the toasted walnut butter:

3   **tablespoons walnuts**

2   **teaspoons walnut oil**

     large pinch of sugar

     salt and freshly ground pepper

2   **tablespoons unsalted butter, at room temperature**

¼   **cup (2 fl oz/60 ml) heavy (double) cream**

     large pinch of freshly grated nutmeg

¼   **cup (2 fl oz/60 ml) fresh orange juice**

     salt and freshly ground pepper

     flat-leaf (Italian) parsley leaves

Acorn Squash Soup with Toasted Walnut Butter

Autumn brings the familiar sight of market stands featuring baskets piled high with winter squashes. In this recipe, butternut, Hubbard, pumpkin, buttercup, or turban can be substituted for the acorn squash.

PREHEAT AN OVEN to 375°F (190°C). Lightly oil a baking sheet.

Cut each squash in half through the stem end and place, cut sides down, on the prepared baking sheet. Bake until easily pierced with a knife, about 45 minutes. Remove from the oven and set aside until cool enough to handle. Using a spoon, scoop out the seeds and fibers and discard. Spoon the flesh into a bowl and set aside. Leave the oven set at 375°F (190°C).

In a soup pot over medium heat, melt the butter. Add the bacon and onion and sauté until the onion is soft, about 10 minutes. Raise the heat to high, add the squash and stock and bring to a gentle boil. Reduce the heat to medium and simmer, uncovered, until the squash disintegrates, about 30 minutes.

Meanwhile, make the walnut butter: In a small bowl, toss together the walnuts, walnut oil, sugar and salt and pepper to taste and spread out on a baking sheet. Toast until golden, 5–7 minutes. Remove from the oven, let cool and chop finely. In a small bowl, using a fork, mash together the walnuts and butter. Season to taste with salt and pepper. Spoon out the butter onto a piece of plastic wrap and, using the plastic wrap, shape into a log about 1 inch (2.5 cm) in diameter. Wrap and refrigerate until serving.

Remove the squash from the heat and let cool for 20 minutes. Using a blender and working in batches, purée the soup on high speed until smooth, 2–3 minutes for each batch. Pass through a fine-mesh sieve into a clean saucepan. Add the cream, nutmeg, orange juice and salt and pepper to taste. Reheat to serving temperature and ladle into warmed bowls. Cut the walnut butter into 6 equal slices and float a slice in each bowl. Garnish with parsley leaves and serve hot. *Serves 6*

Vegetable Barley Soup

2½   qt (2.5 l) chicken or vegetable stock

½   cup (4 oz/125 g) pearl barley

2   carrots, peeled and diced

2   parsnips, peeled and diced

2   boiling potatoes, unpeeled,
diced

1   rutabaga, peeled and diced

1   cup (2 oz/60 g) broccoli
florets

1   teaspoon chopped fresh
thyme

1   teaspoon chopped fresh
oregano

1   tablespoon chopped fresh
flat-leaf (Italian) parsley

Pearl barley is barley from which the hard outer hull and germ have been removed, leaving small, cream-colored balls that look like the gems for which they are named. In this recipe, the tiny grains are used to thicken the soup, resulting in a pleasantly chewy texture.

IN A LARGE SOUP POT over high heat, bring the stock to a boil. Add the barley, reduce the heat to medium-low, cover and simmer until almost tender, 15–20 minutes.

Raise the heat to medium-high and bring to a simmer. Add the carrots, parsnips, potatoes, rutabaga, broccoli, thyme and oregano. Simmer, uncovered, until all the vegetables are tender, about 15 minutes.

Ladle into warmed bowls, garnish with the parsley and serve immediately.
Serves 6

I am...a mushroom
On whom the dew of heaven drops now and then.

—John Ford

Wild Rice and Wild Mushroom Soup

½ cup (3 oz/90 g) wild rice

3 cups (24 fl oz/750 ml) boiling water

½ teaspoon salt, plus salt to taste

½ oz (15 g) dried wild mushrooms such as porcini, chanterelles or shiitakes

2 tablespoons unsalted butter

1 yellow onion, finely chopped

1 celery stalk, finely chopped

½ cup (4 fl oz/125 ml) dry white wine

¾ lb (375 g) fresh button mushrooms, brushed clean and sliced

3 cups (24 fl oz/750 ml) chicken or vegetable stock

½ cup (4 fl oz/125 ml) heavy (double) cream

freshly ground pepper

1 tablespoon chopped fresh flat-leaf (Italian) parsley

Wild rice isn't really a rice at all, but a semiaquatic grass native to North America. In California and Minnesota, wild rice grows throughout the summer and is harvested in September and October. Its earthy flavor makes it a perfect grain for serving during the autumn months.

RINSE THE WILD RICE in several changes of water and drain. Place the rice in a saucepan and add 2 cups (16 fl oz/500 ml) of the boiling water and the ½ teaspoon salt. Place over high heat and bring to a boil. Immediately reduce the heat to low, cover and cook without stirring until tender and the water is absorbed, about 40 minutes. Remove from the heat and let cool.

Meanwhile, place the dried mushrooms in a small bowl and add the remaining 1 cup (8 fl oz/250 ml) boiling water. Let stand for 30 minutes until softened. Drain, reserving the liquid, and set the mushrooms aside. Strain the liquid through a sieve lined with cheesecloth (muslin). Set aside.

In a soup pot over medium heat, melt the butter. Add the onion and celery and sauté, stirring occasionally, until soft, about 10 minutes. Raise the heat to high, add the wine and cook until reduced to about 2 tablespoons, 3–4 minutes. Reduce the heat to medium, add the fresh and rehydrated mushrooms and sauté, stirring occasionally, until the mushrooms wilt, about 15 minutes. Raise the heat to high, add the stock and the reserved mushroom liquid and bring to a boil. Reduce the heat to medium and cook, uncovered, until the mushrooms are very soft, about 20 minutes. Add the wild rice and the cream and simmer for 5 minutes longer to blend the flavors. Season to taste with salt and pepper.

Ladle the soup into warmed bowls and garnish with the parsley. Serve immediately. *Serves 6*

Listen! the wind is rising,
and the air is wild with leaves,
We have had our summer evenings,
now for October eves!

—Humbert Wolfe

White Bean Soup with Smoked Ham

¾ cup (5½ oz/170 g) dried small white (navy), white kidney or cannellini beans

6 fresh parsley sprigs

2 fresh thyme sprigs

2 bay leaves

1 tablespoon olive oil

¼ lb (125 g) bacon, finely diced

1 yellow onion, minced

3 cloves garlic, minced

2 smoked ham hocks, 1 lb (500 g) total weight

1½ cups (9 oz/280 g) peeled, seeded and chopped tomatoes (fresh or canned)

6 cups (48 fl oz/1.5 l) chicken stock

3 tablespoons chopped fresh mint, plus mint sprigs for garnish (optional)

salt and freshly ground pepper

Pantry staples such as beans and smoked meats are traditionally featured in the soups and stews of cold-weather months. In this recipe, a trio of hearty autumn herbs flavors the beans as they cook. Corn bread *(recipe on page 16)* makes a good accompaniment.

PICK OVER THE BEANS and discard any impurities or damaged beans. Rinse the beans, place in a bowl and add water to cover generously. Soak for about 3 hours. Drain and place in a saucepan with the parsley and thyme sprigs, bay leaves and water to cover by about 2 inches (5 cm). Place over medium-high heat, bring to a boil, reduce the heat to low and simmer, uncovered, until nearly tender, 40–50 minutes. Drain well and discard the parsley, thyme and bay leaves.

While the beans are cooking, in a soup pot over medium heat, warm the olive oil. Add the bacon and onion and sauté, stirring occasionally, until the onion is soft, about 10 minutes. Add the garlic and continue to cook for 1 minute. Add the ham hocks, tomatoes and chicken stock and bring to a boil. Reduce the heat to low and cook, uncovered, until the ham just begins to fall from the bone, about 1 hour. Add the beans and continue to simmer until the ham falls from the bones and the beans are very tender, about 1 hour longer.

Remove the ham hocks from the soup and set aside until cool enough to handle. Discard the skin and bones and cut the meat into ½-inch (12-mm) pieces. Add the ham and chopped mint to the soup, stir well and season to taste with salt and pepper.

Ladle the soup into warmed bowls, garnish with mint sprigs if desired, and serve immediately. *Serves 6*

Smoky Eggplant Soup with Red Pepper Cream

2	eggplants (aubergines), 1½ lb (750 g) each
1	red bell pepper (capsicum)
¼	cup (2 fl oz/60 ml) heavy (double) cream
	pinch of cayenne pepper
	salt and freshly ground black pepper
2	tablespoons olive oil
2	yellow onions, coarsely chopped
4	cloves garlic, minced
6	cups (48 fl oz/1.5 l) chicken stock
	flat-leaf (Italian) parsley sprigs

Eggplants reach their peak in late summer and early autumn, when their flesh is dense, firm and sweet and only tiny seeds have developed. Use them as soon as possible after they have been harvested for the best texture and flavor.

PREHEAT AN OVEN to 375°F (190°C).

Using tongs, hold each eggplant over the flame of a gas stove and turn occasionally until blackened on all sides, about 10 minutes. Alternatively, blacken the skins over a charcoal fire. Place the blackened eggplants on a baking sheet. Bake until very tender when pierced with a knife, 10–15 minutes. Remove from the oven and let cool. Peel off the skin and reserve the flesh.

Preheat a broiler (griller). Cut the bell pepper in half lengthwise and remove the stem, seeds and ribs. Place, cut sides down, on a baking sheet and broil (grill) until blackened and blistered. Remove from the broiler and cover loosely with aluminum foil. Let steam until cool enough to handle, 10–15 minutes, then peel off the skin. Transfer the pepper to a blender or a food processor fitted with the metal blade and purée until very smooth. In a small bowl, whisk the cream until soft peaks form. Fold in the pepper purée and season with cayenne pepper, salt and black pepper. Cover and refrigerate.

In a soup pot over medium heat, warm the olive oil. Add the onions and sauté, stirring occasionally, until soft, about 10 minutes. Add the garlic and cook, stirring, for 1 minute. Add the eggplant flesh and the stock, bring to a simmer and simmer, uncovered, until the eggplant falls apart, about 30 minutes. Using a blender and working in batches, purée the soup on high speed until smooth, 3–4 minutes for each batch. Season to taste with salt. If the soup is too thick, add water until it is the consistency of heavy (double) cream.

Ladle into warmed bowls and spoon some red pepper cream over each serving. Garnish with parsley sprigs and serve immediately with any remaining red pepper cream on the side. *Serves 6*

Fennel, Celery, Parsley and Prosciutto Salad

¼	cup (2 fl oz/60 ml) extra-virgin olive oil
3	tablespoons fresh lemon juice
½	teaspoon minced garlic
	salt and freshly ground pepper
3	fennel bulbs
3	celery stalks, cut on the diagonal into thin slices
1	cup (1 oz/30 g) fresh flat-leaf (Italian) parsley leaves
2	oz (60 g) prosciutto, sliced paper-thin

Fennel has a mild anise flavor that is more pronounced when the vegetable is eaten raw than when it is cooked. There are two varieties: Florentine, the type most often found in the market and sometimes mislabeled anise, and common fennel, which produces the brown seeds used as a spice. Look for bulbs that are unblemished and firm to the touch.

IN A SMALL BOWL, whisk together the olive oil, lemon juice, garlic and salt and pepper to taste to form a vinaigrette.

If the fennel bulbs include the stalks and feathery fronds, coarsely chop enough of the feathery fronds to measure about 2 tablespoons. Discard the remaining fronds along with the stalks, or reserve for another use. Remove any damaged outer leaves from the bulbs and discard. Cut the bulbs in half lengthwise and trim away the tough core portions. Using a sharp knife, slice the fennel bulbs lengthwise into paper-thin slices.

In a bowl, combine the fennel, celery, parsley leaves, and the chopped fennel fronds, if using. Drizzle on the vinaigrette and toss to coat all the ingredients evenly. Transfer to a serving platter or individual plates and arrange the prosciutto in curly ribbons on the top. Serve immediately. *Serves 6*

Harvest Fruit Salad

½ cup (2 oz/60 g) pecan halves

1 tablespoon sherry vinegar

1 tablespoon red wine vinegar

1 tablespoon walnut oil

3 tablespoons extra-virgin olive oil

salt and freshly ground pepper

4 pears *(see note)*, 1½ lb (750 g), halved, cored and diced

2 cups (12 oz/375 g) red and green seedless grapes, in any combination

2 green or red apples, such as Cortland, Delicious, Granny Smith, McIntosh or pippin, halved, cored and diced

Pears predate Christianity by two thousand years. The early wild pears were bitter and almost inedible, so grafting methods were introduced to produce more palatable fruits. Since then, some six thousand varieties have been named in Europe and America alone. For this salad, the Bartlett (Williams'), Red Bartlett, Anjou, Seckel or Comice is recommended. Among the grape variety possibilities are Flame, Ruby, Ribier and Thompson. Garnish each serving with thin slices of apple and pear.

PREHEAT AN OVEN to 350°F (180°C). Spread the pecans on a baking sheet and toast until lightly browned and fragrant, 5–7 minutes. Remove from the oven and let cool.

In a small bowl, whisk together the sherry vinegar, red wine vinegar, walnut oil, olive oil and salt and pepper to taste to form a vinaigrette.

In a salad bowl, combine the pears, grapes, apples and pecans. Add the vinaigrette, toss gently to coat and serve. *Serves 6*

Warm Cabbage Salad

2 tablespoons extra-virgin
olive oil

2 large shallots, minced

2–3 lb (1–1.5 kg) assorted
cabbages *(see note),* cored
and cut into shreds ¼ inch
(6 mm) wide

½ teaspoon caraway seeds

2 tart green apples such as
Granny Smith or pippin,
halved, cored and cut into
thin slices

3 tablespoons white wine
vinegar

salt and freshly ground
pepper

¼ cup (¼ oz/7 g) fresh flat-leaf
(Italian) parsley leaves

The word *cabbage* comes from the English corruption of the Old French word *caboche*, meaning "head." The cabbage family is broad, with Brussels sprouts, broccoli, cauliflower, kale, bok choy, and Savoy, napa and celery cabbages among the many relatives. This salad is best made with green, red, napa and Savoy cabbages, in any combination.

IN A LARGE FRYING PAN over medium heat, warm the olive oil. Add the shallots and sauté, stirring occasionally, until soft, about 10 minutes. Add the cabbages and caraway seeds, cover partially and cook, stirring occasionally, until the cabbages just begin to soften, about 10 minutes. Add the apples and vinegar and stir together. Continue to cook, stirring occasionally, until the apples are warm, 1–2 minutes. Season to taste with salt and pepper.

Stir in the parsley leaves and transfer to a warmed serving dish. Serve immediately. *Serves 6*

Salad of Figs, Pomegranates, Persimmons and Pears

½   cup (2 oz/60 g) walnut halves

1   small pomegranate

1½ tablespoons red wine vinegar

3   tablespoons extra-virgin olive oil

   salt and freshly ground pepper

2   large heads frisée, carefully rinsed and stems trimmed

1   Fuyu persimmon, cut into thin slices

1   Red Bartlett pear, halved, cored and cut into thin slices

6   fresh figs, halved through the stem end

The pomegranate tree is small with narrow leaves and bright red hibiscuslike blossoms. Its leathery-skinned, slightly hexagonal fruits are filled with many translucent ruby red seeds that make a nice addition to autumn salads. For this dish, use the tomato-shaped Fuyu persimmon, which has a tender but crisp flesh, and is generally eaten raw.

PREHEAT AN OVEN to 350°F (180°C). Spread the walnuts on a baking sheet and toast until lightly browned and fragrant, 5–7 minutes. Remove from the oven and let cool.

Using a small, sharp knife, score the skin of the pomegranate into quarters. Fill a bowl three-fourths full with water. Holding the pomegranate in the bowl of water, peel off the pomegranate skin, then gently pull the seeds from the membrane, letting them sink to the bottom of the bowl. Scoop out the seeds and let drain on a paper towel.

In a small bowl, whisk together the vinegar, olive oil, and salt and pepper to taste to form a vinaigrette.

Arrange the frisée, sliced persimmon and pear, and fig halves on individual plates, dividing them equally. Garnish with the pomegranate seeds and walnut halves. Drizzle with the vinaigrette and serve. *Serves 4*

My salad days,
When I was green in judgement.

—William Shakespeare

Escarole and Endive Salad with Gorgonzola and Walnuts

½   cup (2 oz/60 g) walnut halves

3   tablespoons extra-virgin olive oil

1   tablespoon walnut oil

2   tablespoons red wine vinegar

1   shallot, minced

    salt and freshly ground pepper

4   heads Belgian endive (chicory/witloof), 1 lb (500 g) total weight, cored and leaves separated

1   head escarole (Batavian endive), ½ lb (250 g), carefully rinsed and torn into 2-inch (5-cm) pieces

3   oz (90 g) Gorgonzola cheese, crumbled

Escarole is part of the chicory family, along with Belgian endive and radicchio. While many vegetables are prized for their delicate flavors, members of this clan are appreciated for their slightly bitter taste. When eaten raw, they pair especially well with more strongly flavored, rich ingredients such as nuts, cheeses and fruits.

PREHEAT AN OVEN to 350°F (180°C). Spread the walnuts on a baking sheet and toast until lightly browned and fragrant, 5–7 minutes. Remove from the oven and let cool.

In a small bowl, whisk together the olive oil, walnut oil, vinegar, shallot and salt and pepper to taste to form a vinaigrette.

In a bowl, combine the endives and escarole. Drizzle on the vinaigrette and toss to coat the leaves evenly. Transfer to a serving platter and garnish with the Gorgonzola and walnuts. Serve immediately. *Serves 6*

main
courses

2	**ducks, 4½–5 lb (2.25–2.5 kg) each**
	salt and freshly ground pepper
1	**orange**
1	**celery stalk, cut into 2-inch (5-cm) pieces**
1	**carrot, cut into 2-inch (5-cm) pieces**
1	**large yellow onion, cut into eighths**
¼	**cup (3 oz/90 g) pure maple syrup**
1	**tablespoon balsamic vinegar**
	orange wedges
	orange zest strip, optional

Maple-Glazed Crispy Duck

Duck season runs from early autumn through the winter months, although pen-raised ducks can be found in specialty butcher shops throughout the year. Most cooks prefer the latter, which are meatier and milder in flavor than the wild bird. If only frozen ducks are available, thaw slowly in the refrigerator or in a basin of cool water.

RINSE THE DUCKS inside and out and pat dry with paper towels. Prick the ducks all over with the tines of a fork, particularly underneath the wing joints along the breast and wherever you see a deposit of fat. Season inside and out with salt and pepper.

Using a vegetable peeler, peel the orange, removing only the colored zest; reserve the zest. Juice the orange and set the juice aside. Divide the orange zest, celery, carrot and onion evenly between the duck cavities. Truss the ducks by tying the legs together with kitchen string. Select a heavy pot large enough to hold the ducks side by side. Pour water into the bottom of the pot to a depth of about 1 inch (2.5 cm). Cover and bring to a boil over high heat. Place the ducks in the pot, breast side up, reduce the heat to low and cover tightly. Cook until the skin of each duck is white and the meat is firm to the touch, 50–60 minutes. Meanwhile, preheat an oven to 425°F (220°C).

When the ducks are ready, transfer them to a roasting pan fitted with a rack, placing them breast side up. Roast for 30 minutes.

In a small bowl, stir together the orange juice, maple syrup and vinegar. Remove the ducks from the oven and brush with some of the orange juice mixture. Reduce the oven temperature to 400°F (200°C) and continue to roast the ducks, basting every 5 minutes with the remaining orange juice mixture, until they are mahogany brown, 25–30 minutes longer. Remove from the oven and transfer to a platter. Cover and let rest for 10 minutes.

Uncover the ducks and garnish with orange wedges and a long strip of orange zest, if desired. Carve the ducks at the table, removing the legs, then slicing the breast meat. *Serves 6–8*

Coq au Vin with Autumn Vegetables

2   tablespoons unsalted butter, at room temperature

¼   lb (125 g) bacon, cut into small dice

1   chicken, 4 lb (2 kg), cut into 12 serving pieces

       salt and freshly ground pepper

4   cups (32 fl oz/1 l) dry red wine such as Cabernet Sauvignon or Côtes-du-Rhône

4   cups (32 fl oz/1 l) chicken stock

1   tablespoon tomato paste

3   cloves garlic, minced

2   bay leaves

½   teaspoon chopped fresh thyme

6   fresh parsley sprigs, tied together with kitchen string, plus 1 tablespoon coarsely chopped parsley

2   parsnips, peeled and cut into 1-inch (2.5-cm) lengths

2   carrots, peeled and cut into 1-inch (2.5-cm) lengths

1   turnip, peeled and cut into wedges

1   rutabaga (swede), peeled and cut into wedges

3   tablespoons all-purpose (plain) flour

Root vegetables come in a range of colors, shapes and sizes. If you like, substitute baby root vegetables for the regular-sized ones called for here.

IN A LARGE, HEAVY POT over medium heat, melt 1 tablespoon of the butter. Add the bacon and cook, stirring occasionally, until lightly golden, about 10 minutes. Using a slotted spoon, transfer to a plate.

Rinse the chicken pieces and pat dry with paper towels. Sprinkle on all sides with salt and pepper. Raise the heat to medium-high and, working in batches, add the chicken pieces to the pot. Cook, turning as necessary, until lightly golden, about 10 minutes. When all of the chicken is golden, return the pieces to the pot along with the bacon. Raise the heat to high and add the wine, stock, tomato paste, garlic, bay leaves, chopped thyme and parsley sprigs. Bring to a boil, reduce the heat to low, cover and simmer until the chicken juices run clear when a thigh is pierced, 25–30 minutes. Using tongs, transfer the chicken to a large shallow dish and keep warm.

Strain the liquid through a fine-mesh sieve and return it to the pot. Place over high heat and add the parsnips, carrots, turnip and rutabaga. Bring to a boil, reduce the heat to medium-low, cover and simmer until the vegetables are tender, about 15 minutes. Using a slotted spoon, transfer the vegetables to the dish holding the chicken.

In a small bowl, using a fork, mix the flour and the remaining 1 tablespoon butter to form a paste. Bring the liquid in the pot to a boil over high heat and whisk in the flour-butter mixture. Reduce the heat to medium and simmer, stirring occasionally, until the liquid lightly coats a spoon, 2–3 minutes.

To serve, add the chicken and vegetables to the pot and heat through. Using the slotted spoon, transfer the vegetables and chicken to a warmed platter. Drizzle with the sauce and garnish with the chopped parsley. *Serves 6*

Braised Game Hens with Grapes and Late-Harvest Riesling

6   Cornish game hens, about
     1¼ lb (625 g) each

8   fresh thyme sprigs, plus
     thyme sprigs for garnish

1½   cups (12 fl oz/375 ml) late-
     harvest Riesling

2   tablespoons unsalted butter

1   small yellow onion, coarsely
     chopped

1   carrot, peeled and coarsely
     chopped

4   cups (32 fl oz/1 l) chicken
     stock

1   teaspoon cornstarch (corn-
     flour)

2   tablespoons water

¼   teaspoon sherry vinegar

     salt and freshly ground
     pepper

2   cups (12 oz/375 g) green and
     red seedless grapes such as
     Thompson, Flame, Ruby
     and Champagne, in any
     combination

Late-harvest Riesling is made from grapes left on the vine a little longer than normal. They begin to resemble raisins in both sweetness and appearance, and the resulting wine has a delightful spicy-sweet quality.

RINSE THE GAME HENS, pat dry with paper towels and cut in half through the breastbone. Place them in a large, shallow nonaluminum bowl with the 8 thyme sprigs and the Riesling. Cover and refrigerate for 12 hours.

Remove the hens from the marinade. Strain the marinade through a fine-mesh sieve into a bowl and set aside. Dry the hens with paper towels.

In a large frying pan over medium-high heat, melt the butter. Add the onion and carrot and sauté until golden, 10–12 minutes. Using a slotted spoon, transfer to a plate. Working in batches, add the hen halves to the pan, skin side down, and cook, turning once, until golden on both sides, 8–10 minutes total. Return the onion and carrot to the pan along with the strained marinade and the stock. Bring to a boil, reduce the heat to low, cover and simmer until the hens are tender, about 25 minutes.

Using tongs, transfer the hens to a warmed platter and cover to keep warm. Strain the cooking liquid through a fine-mesh sieve into a clean container and, using a spoon, skim off any fat from the surface. Return the strained liquid to the frying pan and place over high heat. Bring to a boil and boil until the liquid is reduced by half, 5–10 minutes. In a small bowl, stir together the cornstarch and water. Whisk the cornstarch-water mixture into the reduced liquid and boil, whisking constantly, until the liquid lightly coats a spoon, about 30 seconds. Add the vinegar and season to taste with salt and pepper. Reduce the heat to medium, return the hens to the pan and add the grapes. Cover and cook until heated through, 3–4 minutes.

Using a slotted spoon, transfer the hens and grapes to the platter. Spoon the sauce over the top, garnish with thyme sprigs and serve. *Serves 6*

Pork Tenderloin with Cider Glaze and Dried Fruits

2   **large pork tenderloins, 2½ lb (1.25 kg) total weight, trimmed of excess fat**

1   **tablespoon olive oil**

¼   **teaspoon sweet paprika**

¼   **teaspoon ground cumin**

    large pinch of cayenne pepper

¼   **teaspoon ground cloves**

¼   **teaspoon salt, plus salt to taste**

    freshly ground pepper

⅓   **cup (2 oz/60 g) dried apricots, coarsely chopped**

⅓   **cup (2 oz/60 g) dried pears, coarsely chopped**

3   **tablespoons golden raisins (sultanas)**

1½   **tablespoons sherry vinegar or white wine vinegar**

1   **teaspoon sugar**

1¼   **cups (10 fl oz/310 ml) water**

3   **cups (24 fl oz/750 ml) apple cider**

2   **bay leaves**

4   **whole cloves**

1½   **cups (12 fl oz/375 ml) chicken stock**

There are two types of apple cider: "sweet," which is freshly pressed, and "hard," which has fermented and has an alcohol content. Use sweet here.

BUTTERFLY THE PORK TENDERLOINS: Slice each tenderloin lengthwise, cutting almost all of the way through. Open flat and then flatten slightly by pounding with a meat pounder. In a small bowl, stir together the oil, paprika, cumin, cayenne, cloves, the ¼ teaspoon salt and the pepper to taste and rub over the pork. Place in a baking dish, cover and refrigerate for 1 hour.

Meanwhile, in a small saucepan, combine the apricots, pears, raisins, vinegar, sugar and water and bring to a boil. Reduce the heat to low, cover and simmer until the fruit softens, about 20 minutes. Uncover and cook over high heat until the liquid is reduced by half, about 10 minutes. Remove from the heat.

Using a slotted spoon, lift out the fruits, reserving the liquid. Divide the fruits evenly between the 2 pieces of pork, spreading them over the meat in an even layer. Roll up each tenderloin into its original shape, enclosing the filling in a spiral, and tie at 1-inch (2.5-cm) intervals with kitchen string.

In a sauté pan over high heat, bring the cider and the reserved poaching liquid to a boil. Boil until reduced by three fourths, about 15 minutes. Add the bay leaves, cloves and stock and return to a boil. Add the pork tenderloins and reduce the heat to medium-low. Cover and simmer until the pork is firm to the touch and slightly pink when cut into with a knife, 20–25 minutes.

Transfer the tenderloins to a cutting board and cover to keep warm. Raise the heat to high and boil until the liquid is reduced by half and thickens slightly, about 5 minutes. Strain through a fine-mesh sieve into a small bowl, season to taste with salt and pepper and cover to keep warm.

Snip the strings and cut the pork into slices ½ inch (12 mm) thick. Arrange on a warmed platter, drizzle with the sauce and serve. *Serves 6*

The turkey…is a much more respectable bird,
and withal a true original native of America.

—Benjamin Franklin

Roast Turkey with Dried Apple and Corn Bread Stuffing

1   turkey, 10–12 lb (5–6 kg), with the giblets

    salt and ground pepper

6   cups (48 fl oz/1.5 l) chicken stock

1   yellow onion, diced

1   carrot, peeled and diced

6   fresh parsley sprigs, ¼ teaspoon dried thyme and 1 bay leaf

For the stuffing:

¾   cup (6 oz/185 g) unsalted butter

2   large yellow onions, finely diced

4   celery stalks, finely diced

1   cup (3 oz/90 g) dried apples, coarsely chopped

¼   cup (⅓ oz/10 g) chopped fresh flat-leaf (Italian) parsley

1   tablespoon each chopped fresh thyme and sage

    corn bread *(recipe on page 16)*, air-dried for 2 days, cubed

    salt and freshly ground pepper

1   tablespoon all-purpose (plain) flour

1   teaspoon cornstarch (corn-flour)

RINSE THE TURKEY and giblets and pat dry. Rub the turkey inside and out with 2 teaspoons salt. Place the giblets in a saucepan and add the stock, onion, carrot and herbs. Bring to a boil, reduce the heat to low and simmer until reduced by three-fourths, about 1½ hours. Strain through a fine-mesh sieve.

To make the stuffing, in a large frying pan over medium heat, melt ½ cup (4 oz/125 g) of the butter. Add the onions and celery and sauté until soft, about 10 minutes. Transfer to a bowl and add the apples, parsley, thyme, sage, corn bread and about 1½ cups (12 fl oz/375 ml) of the stock. Stir until well mixed, light and fluffy. Season with salt and pepper. Preheat an oven to 400°F (200°C).

Stuff the body and neck cavity loosely with the stuffing, then truss as directed on page 14. Place, breast side up, on an oiled rack in a roasting pan; tuck the wing tips under the breast. Melt the remaining ¼ cup (2 oz/60 g) butter and brush 1 tablespoon on the turkey. Soak a double layer of cheesecloth (muslin) large enough to cover the turkey in the remaining butter.

Roast for 45 minutes. Reduce the heat to 325°F (165°C). Drape the soaked cheesecloth over the turkey (see page 14) and continue to roast, basting every 30 minutes, until the juices run clear when the thickest part of the thigh is pricked or an instant-read thermometer inserted into the thigh registers 180°F (82°C), 1½–2 hours longer. Remove from the oven and let stand for 20 minutes. Discard the cheesecloth and transfer the turkey to a platter.

Reserve 2 tablespoons fat and drippings in the pan (discard the rest) and place over high heat. In a cup, whisk together the flour, cornstarch and ½ cup (4 fl oz/125 ml) of the stock, then whisk into the pan. Add the remaining stock and stir until thickened, about 2 minutes. Simmer for 1 minute longer and strain through a fine-mesh sieve into a sauceboat; keep warm.

Snip the trussing string. Carve the turkey (see page 14) and spoon the stuffing into a serving dish at the table. Pass the gravy. *Serves 8*

Too few people understand a really good sandwich.

—James Beard

Turkey Sandwich with Tapenade and Fontina

For the tapenade:

1 clove garlic, minced

½ cup (2½ oz/75 g) pitted Niçoise olives

1 tablespoon drained capers, chopped

2 anchovy fillets, soaked in water to cover for 5 minutes, drained and patted dry

1 tablespoon fresh lemon juice

1 tablespoon extra-virgin olive oil

freshly ground pepper

6 slices country-style bread

1 tablespoon extra-virgin olive oil

1 clove garlic

1½ lb (750 g) roasted turkey, thickly sliced

6 oz (185 g) Fontina cheese, shredded

Here is a delectable use for leftover holiday turkey. Serve this sandwich for lunch or with a soup or salad for a light dinner main course. The bread can also be grilled over a charcoal fire for a smokier flavor.

To make the tapenade, place the garlic and three-fourths of the olives in a food processor fitted with the metal blade. Process until the mixture forms a chunky paste. Add the capers and anchovies and pulse 4 or 5 times to mix. Add the remaining olives and pulse 4 or 5 times until a chunky paste again forms. Transfer to a bowl. Stir in the lemon juice and the olive oil and season to taste with pepper. You should have about ⅔ cup (5 oz/155 g).

Preheat a broiler (griller).

Lightly brush the bread slices on both sides with the olive oil. Arrange in a single layer on a baking sheet. Place in the broiler 4–6 inches (10–15 cm) from the heat source and broil (grill), turning once, until lightly golden on both sides, 30–60 seconds on each side. Rub both sides of each piece of toast lightly with the garlic clove. Divide the tapenade evenly among the bread slices and spread to cover one side of each slice completely. Distribute the turkey evenly among the bread slices. Top with the cheese, again dividing evenly.

Return the pan to the broiler (griller) and broil (grill) until the cheese melts, 30–60 seconds. Serve immediately. *Serves 6*

Awake, O north wind; and come, thou south;
blow upon my garden, that the spices thereof
may flow out.

—Song of Solomon

Crispy Salmon with Spiced Lentils

1½	cups (10½ oz/330 g) lentils
8	whole cloves
1	small yellow onion
2	bay leaves
2	tablespoons extra-virgin olive oil
1	small red (Spanish) onion, minced
4	cloves garlic, minced
3	tomatoes, peeled, seeded and chopped (fresh or canned)
1½	cups (12 fl oz/375 ml) bottled clam juice
1½	teaspoons ground cumin
1½	teaspoons ground ginger
¾	teaspoon ground turmeric
¾	teaspoon sweet paprika
¼	teaspoon cayenne pepper
⅓	cup (½ oz/15 g) chopped fresh flat-leaf (Italian) parsley
⅓	cup (½ oz/15 g) chopped fresh cilantro (fresh coriander)
3	tablespoons fresh lemon juice
	salt and freshly ground pepper
6	salmon fillets, each 5–6 oz (155–185 g) and ¾–1 inch (2–2.5 cm) thick, skinned
	lemon wedges

For a thousand years, tiny, lens-shaped lentils have been popular in many European countries and a staple throughout the Middle East and India. They are a natural partner to fresh salmon. Small lentils from Le Puy, France, are particularly prized, although ordinary brown lentils also work well here.

PICK OVER THE LENTILS and discard any impurities or damaged lentils. Rinse well and place in a large saucepan. Add water to cover by 2 inches (5 cm). Stick the cloves into the yellow onion and add to the saucepan along with the bay leaves. Bring to a boil over high heat, reduce the heat to medium-low and simmer, uncovered, until the lentils are tender, 15–20 minutes. Drain and discard the onion and bay leaves. Set the lentils aside.

In a large frying pan over medium heat, warm 1 tablespoon of the olive oil. Add the red onion and sauté, stirring occasionally, until soft, about 10 minutes. Add the garlic, tomatoes, clam juice, cumin, ginger, turmeric, paprika and cayenne and cook uncovered, stirring occasionally, until the tomatoes are soft, about 3 minutes. Add the parsley, cilantro and lentils and cook, stirring occasionally, until the lentils are hot, about 2 minutes. Stir in the lemon juice and season to taste with salt and pepper. Keep warm.

Preheat a ridged cast-iron stove-top grill pan over high heat until very hot, about 15 minutes. Brush the salmon with the remaining 1 tablespoon olive oil and place on the pan. Cook until golden and crisp on one side, 4–5 minutes. Turn over the salmon, sprinkle with salt and pepper and continue to cook until opaque throughout, 3–4 minutes longer. Alternatively, prepare a fire in a charcoal grill. Brush the salmon with oil as directed and grill about 4 inches (10 cm) from the fire for 4–5 minutes on each side.

To serve, spoon the warm lentils onto a warmed serving platter. Place the salmon fillets in the center and garnish with lemon wedges. Serve at once.

Serves 6

Polenta with Sausages and Tomato-Olive Ragout

6   cups (2¼ lb/1.1 kg) peeled, seeded and chopped tomatoes (fresh or canned)

1   small red (Spanish) onion, peeled

4   cloves garlic

    salt and freshly ground pepper

2   lb (1 kg) Italian pork sausages, preferably flavored with fennel seeds

8½ cups (68 fl oz/2.1 l) water

2   cups (12 oz/375 g) polenta

2   teaspoons chopped fresh rosemary

3   tablespoons unsalted butter

¾   cup (4 oz/125 g) pitted brine-cured black olives such as Kalamata or Niçoise

    wedge of Parmesan cheese for shaving

1½ tablespoons coarsely chopped fresh flat-leaf (Italian) parsley

A staple of northern Italy, polenta has a hearty character best accented by robust flavors such as the savory ragout paired with it here.

IN A HEAVY SOUP POT over high heat, combine the tomatoes, onion and garlic cloves. Bring to a boil, reduce the heat to low and simmer, uncovered, until the sauce thickens, 45–60 minutes. Remove from the heat and discard the onion. Pass the mixture through the fine disk of a food mill placed over a clean saucepan. Alternatively, purée in a food processor fitted with the metal blade, then pass through a fine-mesh sieve. Season with salt and pepper.

Meanwhile, prick the sausages in several places with a fork. In a large saucepan, bring ½ cup (4 fl oz/125 ml) of the water to a boil. Add the sausages and cook over medium-high heat, turning occasionally, until golden on all sides and half-cooked, 10–12 minutes. Drain and, when cool enough to handle, cut each sausage on the diagonal into 2-inch (5-cm) pieces.

In a large, heavy saucepan, bring the remaining 8 cups (64 fl oz/2 l) water to a boil over high heat. Slowly add the polenta in a steady stream while whisking constantly. Continue to whisk until the mixture thickens, 3–4 minutes. Switch to a wooden spoon, reduce the heat to medium and continue to simmer, stirring, until the polenta pulls away from the sides of the pan, 20–25 minutes. Stir in the rosemary and butter. Season to taste with salt and pepper.

Meanwhile, place the puréed sauce over medium heat and bring to a simmer. Add the sausage pieces and the olives and simmer, uncovered, until the sausages are cooked through, about 10 minutes.

Divide the polenta equally among warmed individual plates. Spoon the sauce and sausages around the edges. Using a cheese shaver or a vegetable peeler, shave a few pieces of the Parmesan cheese over each serving. Garnish with the parsley and serve immediately. *Serves 6*

They eat, they drink, and in communion sweet
Quaff immortality and joy.

—John Milton

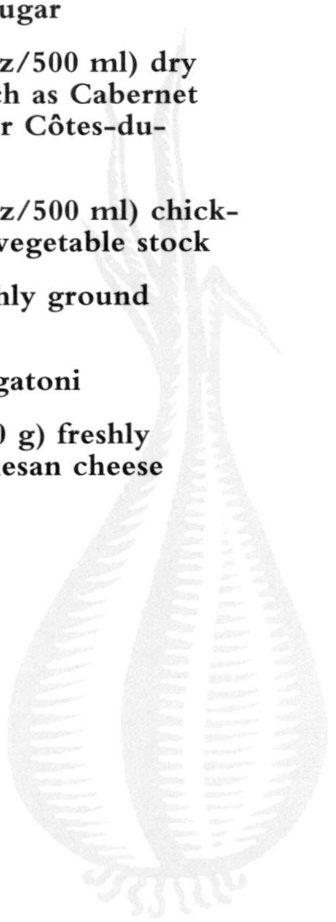

Rigatoni with Caramelized Shallots, Pancetta and Parmesan

- **2 tablespoons extra-virgin olive oil**
- **¼ lb (125 g) pancetta, finely diced**
- **30 small shallots**
- **1 tablespoon sugar**
- **2 cups (16 fl oz/500 ml) dry red wine such as Cabernet Sauvignon or Côtes-du-Rhône**
- **2 cups (16 fl oz/500 ml) chicken stock or vegetable stock**
- **salt and freshly ground pepper**
- **1 lb (500 g) rigatoni**
- **¾ cup (3 oz/90 g) freshly grated Parmesan cheese**

Although shallots are a member of the onion family, they have their own distinctive flavor. They are at their best in the summer and autumn; use the smallest ones you can find. If shallots are unavailable, substitute pearl onions.

In a large frying pan over medium-high heat, warm the olive oil. Add the pancetta and cook, stirring occasionally, until lightly golden, 10–12 minutes. Reduce the heat to medium-low and add the shallots. Cook uncovered, stirring occasionally with a wooden spoon and pressing on the shallots slightly to separate the layers, until golden brown, 25–30 minutes. Add the sugar, stir well and cook until the sugar dissolves, about 4 minutes. Add the wine and stock, bring to a simmer, reduce the heat to medium-low and cook gently until the shallots are very soft and only ½ cup (4 fl oz/125 g) of liquid remains, 30–40 minutes. Season to taste with salt and plenty of pepper.

Just before the shallot sauce is ready, bring a large pot three-fourths full of salted water to a boil. Add the rigatoni and cook until al dente (tender but firm to the bite), 10–12 minutes or according to the package directions. Drain and return the pasta to the pot. Add the shallot sauce and mix well.

To serve, transfer the sauced rigatoni to a warmed serving bowl. Sprinkle with the Parmesan and serve immediately. *Serves 6*

Squash Ravioli with Hazelnut Butter and Parmesan

1	winter squash such as Hubbard, butternut or turban, about 2 lb (1 kg)
¾	cup (1½ oz/45 g) fresh bread crumbs
2	tablespoons plus ¼ cup (1 oz/30 g) freshly grated Parmesan cheese
2	teaspoons honey
½	teaspoon chopped fresh thyme
½	teaspoon chopped fresh rosemary
½	teaspoon chopped fresh sage, plus whole leaves for garnish
1	teaspoon grated orange zest
	salt and freshly ground pepper
1	teaspoon extra-virgin olive oil
2	oz (60 g) prosciutto, thinly sliced, then cut into long strips ¼ inch (6 mm) wide
1	teaspoon walnut oil or hazelnut oil
⅓	cup (2 oz/60 g) hazelnuts (filberts), chopped
6	tablespoons (3 oz/90 g) unsalted butter
	pinch of freshly grated nutmeg
1	lb (500 g) purchased fresh thin egg pasta sheets

PREHEAT AN OVEN to 350°F (180°C). Lightly oil a baking sheet.

Cut the squash in half through the stem end and place, cut side down, on the prepared baking sheet. Bake until easily pierced with a knife, 50–60 minutes. Remove from the oven and set aside until cool enough to handle. Using a spoon, scoop out the seeds and fibers and discard. Spoon the flesh into a bowl. Mash with a potato masher (or pulse a few times in a food processor fitted with the metal blade) until smooth. Add the bread crumbs, the 2 tablespoons Parmesan, the honey, thyme, rosemary, chopped sage and orange zest. Mix well and season to taste with salt and pepper.

In a small frying pan over medium heat, warm the olive oil. Add the prosciutto and sauté until lightly golden, 4–5 minutes. Using a slotted spoon, transfer to a plate. Add the nut oil and hazelnuts to the pan and cook, stirring often, until lightly golden, about 3 minutes. Transfer to the plate and set aside.

In a saucepan over medium-high heat, melt the butter until it turns brown and just begins to smoke, 3–4 minutes. Remove immediately from the heat and add the nutmeg. Set aside.

Place a pasta sheet on a lightly floured work surface. Spoon mounds of filling onto the sheet, spacing them about 1½ inches (4 cm) apart. With a spray mister filled with water, lightly mist around the mounds of filling. Place a second sheet of pasta over the first, covering the mounds, and press around the edges and between the mounds to seal. Using a fluted cutting wheel, cut between the rows of ravioli. Repeat with the remaining pasta sheets and filling.

Bring a large pot three-fourths full of salted water to a boil. Add the ravioli and cook until tender, 2–3 minutes. To serve, reheat the brown butter. Drain the ravioli and place in a warmed serving bowl. Toss with the butter and sprinkle with the prosciutto, hazelnuts and the ¼ cup (1 oz/30 g) Parmesan. Garnish with the sage leaves and serve immediately. *Serves 6–8*

Braised Lamb Shanks with White Beans

1½ cups (10½ oz/330 g) dried small white (navy), white kidney or cannellini beans

2 tablespoons extra-virgin olive oil

6 lamb shanks, ½–¾ lb (250–375 g) each

1 yellow onion, finely diced

1 celery stalk, finely diced

2 large carrots, peeled and finely diced

6 cloves garlic, minced

1½ cups (12 fl oz/375 ml) dry red wine such as Côtes-du-Rhône, Cabernet Sauvignon or Chianti

1½ cups (12 fl oz/375 ml) chicken stock

1½ cups (9 oz/280 g) peeled, seeded and chopped tomatoes (fresh or canned)

3 tablespoons tomato paste

1 teaspoon chopped fresh thyme

1 bay leaf

salt and freshly ground pepper

1 tablespoon shredded lemon zest

2 tablespoons chopped fresh flat-leaf (Italian) parsley

Lamb shanks, white beans, tomatoes and red wine are an ideal union for a hearty autumn dinner. You can substitute the same amount of veal shanks for the lamb shanks, if you like.

PICK OVER THE BEANS and discard any impurities or damaged beans. Rinse the beans, place in a bowl and add water to cover generously. Soak for about 3 hours. Drain and place in a saucepan with water to cover by about 2 inches (5 cm). Place over medium-high heat and bring to a boil. Reduce the heat to low and simmer, uncovered, until nearly tender, 45–60 minutes. Drain well.

Meanwhile, in a deep, heavy pot over medium heat, warm the olive oil. Add the lamb shanks and brown on all sides, 10–12 minutes. Transfer the shanks to a plate. Add the onion, celery and carrots to the pan and sauté over medium heat, stirring occasionally, until the onion is soft, about 10 minutes. Add the garlic and cook, stirring, for 1 minute. Add the wine, stock, tomatoes, tomato paste, thyme, bay leaf and lamb shanks. Bring to a boil over high heat. Reduce the heat to low, cover and simmer until the shanks can be easily pierced with a skewer, 1½–2 hours.

Add the beans, stir well, cover and simmer gently until the lamb begins to fall from the bone and the beans are tender, about 30 minutes longer. Season to taste with salt and pepper. Remove the bay leaf and discard.

In a small bowl, stir together the lemon zest and parsley. Transfer the lamb shanks and beans to individual plates and garnish with the zest-parsley mixture. Serve immediately. *Serves 6*

Papa, potatoes, poultry, prunes and prism,
all very good words for the lips: especially
prunes and prism.

—Charles Dickens

Lamb Chops with Prune Chutney

For the prune chutney:

¼ cup (2 oz/60 g) firmly packed brown sugar

¼ cup (2 fl oz/60 ml) sherry vinegar

1 cup (8 fl oz/250 ml) water

½ teaspoon grated orange zest

2 tablespoons fresh orange juice

   pinch of cayenne pepper

¼ teaspoon salt

1½ cups (9 oz/280 g) pitted prunes, stems removed

2 tablespoons crystallized ginger, finely diced

12 loin lamb chops, each about ¼ lb (125 g) and 1 inch (2.5 cm) thick

2 tablespoons olive oil

   salt and freshly ground pepper

Prune plums, sometimes known as Italian plums or French plums, are picked at the height of their season during the summer months and soon after are dried into prunes. This chutney can be made up to 3 weeks in advance and stored in the refrigerator until ready to use. Any combination of dried fruits can be used in place of the prunes, including apples, figs, golden or dark raisins, pears or apricots. Garnish with shredded orange zest, if you like.

TO MAKE THE CHUTNEY, in a saucepan over medium heat, combine the brown sugar, vinegar, water, orange zest, orange juice, cayenne and salt. Bring to a boil, stirring to dissolve the sugar. Reduce the heat to low and simmer, uncovered, until the mixture thickens slightly, about 20 minutes.

Add the prunes and ginger and continue to cook uncovered over medium heat, stirring occasionally, until the fruit is tender but not mushy and the syrup is thick, about 1 hour. If the mixture begins to dry out during cooking, stir in a little water. Remove from the heat and let cool. You should have about 1½ cups (15 oz/470 g).

Prepare a fire in a charcoal grill, or preheat a broiler (griller).

Brush the lamb chops on both sides with the olive oil and sprinkle on all sides with salt and pepper. Place the lamb chops on a grill rack or on a broiler pan. Grill or broil 4 inches (10 cm) from the heat until browned on the first side, about 5 minutes. Turn and continue to cook until browned on the second side and medium-rare in the center, about 5 minutes longer, or until done to your liking. Transfer 2 lamb chops to each individual plate. Serve immediately, garnished with a spoonful of chutney on the side. *Serves 6*

A runnable stag, a kingly crop.

—John Davidson

3 lb (1.5 kg) boneless venison
   such as rump pot roast, sir-
   loin tip or top round, cut
   into 1½-inch (4-cm) cubes

2 tablespoons all-purpose
   (plain) flour

2 tablespoons olive oil

3 oz (90 g) pancetta, finely
   chopped

1 yellow onion, finely chopped

6 fresh parsley sprigs

3 fresh thyme sprigs

2 bay leaves

4 cloves garlic, minced

1½ cups (12 fl oz/375 ml) dry
   red wine such as Barolo,
   Cabernet Sauvignon or
   Côtes-du-Rhône

4 cups (32 fl oz/1 l) chicken,
   beef or veal stock

1 tablespoon tomato paste

1 lb (500 g) pearl onions

2 tablespoons unsalted butter

1 lb (500 g) small fresh button
   mushrooms, brushed clean

2 tablespoons chopped fresh
   flat-leaf (Italian) parsley

   salt and freshly ground
   pepper

Oven-Braised Venison Ragout

Although meats that are evenly and lightly marbled with fat are generally best for braised and stewed dishes, venison, which is quite lean, makes a tasty ragout.

PREHEAT AN OVEN to 350°F (180°C). Place the venison in a bowl, sprinkle with the flour and toss together.

In a heavy stew pot over medium heat, warm 1 tablespoon of the oil. Add the pancetta and onion and sauté until the onion is soft, about 10 minutes. Using a slotted spoon, transfer to a plate. Raise the heat to medium-high and add the remaining 1 tablespoon oil. Working in batches, add the venison and cook, turning occasionally, until golden brown on all sides, 10–15 minutes. Using kitchen string, tie the herb sprigs and bay leaves into a bundle. Return the onion and pancetta to the pan along with the herb bundle and the garlic. Raise the heat to high and pour in the wine. Bring to a boil, scraping up any browned bits, and boil until the wine is reduced by half, about 5 minutes. Add the stock and the tomato paste and bring to a boil. Cover, place in the oven and cook until the venison can be easily pierced with a knife, about 1½ hours.

Meanwhile, peel the pearl onions: In a saucepan, combine the onions with water to cover. Bring to a boil and boil for 2 minutes. Drain, rinse and drain again. Trim off the root end of each onion, then cut a shallow X into each trimmed end. Squeeze each onion gently to slip off the skin. Set aside.

Melt 1 tablespoon of the butter in a frying pan over medium-high heat. Add the mushrooms and cook, stirring occasionally, until lightly golden, about 10 minutes. Transfer to a plate. Melt the remaining 1 tablespoon butter in the same pan. Add the pearl onions and cook over medium heat, stirring occasionally, until lightly golden, about 10 minutes. Set aside.

When the venison is tender, remove it from the oven and add the onions. Place over medium heat and bring to a simmer. Cook, uncovered, until the onions are tender, about 20 minutes. Add the mushrooms and stir to heat through. Discard the herb bundle. Stir in the chopped parsley and season to taste with salt and pepper. Serve immediately. *Serves 6*

side
dishes

Spaghetti Squash with Brown Butter and Parmesan

1   **spaghetti squash, 2½–3 lb (1.25–1.5 kg)**

¼   **cup (2 oz/60 g) unsalted butter**

pinch of freshly grated nutmeg

⅓   **cup (1½ oz/45 g) freshly grated Parmesan cheese**

salt and freshly ground pepper

Spaghetti squash derives its name from the nature of its flesh: once it is cooked and cut in half, the flesh can be separated into strands that recall the famed Italian pasta. The squash's delicate flavor requires only subtle enhancement.

PLACE THE WHOLE SQUASH in a large pot and add water to cover. Bring to a boil over high heat, reduce the heat to medium-low, and simmer, uncovered, until it can be easily pierced with a knife, about 45 minutes.

Meanwhile, in a saucepan over medium-high heat, melt the butter and cook it until it turns brown and just begins to smoke, 3–4 minutes. Remove immediately from the heat and stir in the nutmeg.

When the squash is done, drain and set aside until cool enough to handle. Cut the squash in half lengthwise and, using a fork, scrape out the seeds and discard. Place the squash halves, cut sides up, on a serving platter and, using the fork, scrape the flesh free of the skin, carefully separating it into the spaghettilike strands that it naturally forms. Leave the strands mounded in the squash halves. If the butter has cooled, place over medium heat until hot.

To serve, drizzle the butter evenly over the squash. Sprinkle with the Parmesan cheese and season to taste with salt and pepper. Serve immediately.

Serves 6

Roasted Squash Purée with Ginger

1   butternut squash, 2½–3 lb (1.25–1.5 kg)

2   tablespoons unsalted butter, at room temperature

½   cup (4 fl oz/125 ml) milk

1½ teaspoons peeled and grated fresh ginger

    salt and freshly ground pepper

A bowl of creamy squash purée is one of the comfort foods of the autumn table. Although squash is often boiled, roasting brings out its sweetness. Acorn, Hubbard, turban squash or pumpkin can be used in place of the butternut squash.

PREHEAT AN OVEN to 400°F (200°C). Lightly oil a baking sheet.

Cut the squash in half through the stem end and place, cut sides down, on the prepared baking sheet. Bake until easily pierced with a knife, 45–50 minutes. Remove from the oven and set aside until cool enough to handle. Using a spoon, scoop out the seeds and fibers and discard. Spoon the flesh into a bowl and keep warm.

In a small saucepan over medium heat, combine the butter and milk and heat until the butter melts and the milk is hot, about 1 minute. Remove from the heat.

Using a potato masher, mash the squash until smooth. Alternatively, process the squash in a food processor fitted with the metal blade, pulsing several times until smooth, about 1 minute. Stir in the milk mixture and ginger and season to taste with salt and pepper.

Transfer to a heavy saucepan and place over low heat. Reheat gently, stirring to prevent scorching. Spoon into a warmed serving bowl and serve immediately. *Serves 6*

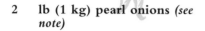

Good sooth, she is
The queen of curds and cream.

—William Shakespeare

2	**lb (1 kg) pearl onions** *(see note)*
4	**tablespoons (2 oz/60 g) unsalted butter**
1	**yellow onion, minced**
1	**teaspoon chopped fresh thyme**
2½	**tablespoons all-purpose (plain) flour**
½	**cup (4 fl oz/125 ml) milk**
½	**cup (4 fl oz/125 ml) heavy (double) cream**
¼	**teaspoon freshly grated nutmeg**
	salt and freshly ground pepper
¾	**cup (3 oz/90 g) fine dried white bread crumbs**

Creamy Pearl Onions

Creamed onions are a seasonal favorite, especially on the holiday table. Pearl onions, traditionally any white onion less than 1½ inches (4 cm) in diameter, are best for this dish. A number of different-colored pearl onions are available at markets today, including white, yellow and purple.

BRING A SAUCEPAN half full of water to a boil over high heat. Add the pearl onions and cook for 2 minutes. Using a slotted spoon, scoop out the onions, rinse with cold water and drain. Reserve the water in the pot. Trim off the ends of each onion, then cut a shallow X into each trimmed end. Squeeze each onion gently to slip off the skin.

Bring the water back to a boil. Add the onions, reduce the heat to low and simmer, uncovered, until soft when pierced with a knife, 15–20 minutes. Using the slotted spoon, transfer the onions to a bowl. Continue to boil the cooking liquid until reduced to 1 cup (8 fl oz/250 ml), 15–20 minutes.

Position an oven rack in the upper part of an oven and preheat to 375°F (190°C).

In a saucepan over medium heat, melt 3 tablespoons of the butter. Add the minced onion and thyme and cook, stirring occasionally, until soft, about 7 minutes. Add the flour and cook, stirring constantly with a wooden spoon, until well mixed and bubbling, about 2 minutes. Add the reserved 1 cup (8 fl oz/250 ml) cooking liquid, the milk and the cream. Cook over medium heat until the sauce boils and thickens slightly, 3–4 minutes. Add the nutmeg and season to taste with salt and pepper. Add the pearl onions, adjust the heat to a gentle simmer and cook until the onions are hot, about 3 minutes.

Transfer the onion mixture to a 2-qt (2-l) baking dish and sprinkle the bread crumbs evenly over the top. Cut the remaining 1 tablespoon butter into 6 equal pieces and dot the bread crumbs evenly with the butter. Bake until the crumbs are golden and small bubbles appear along the edges of the dish, 15–20 minutes. Serve immediately. *Serves 6*

Braised Fennel with Olive Oil and Garlic

4	fennel bulbs, about 2 lb (1 kg) total weight
3	tablespoons extra-virgin olive oil
3	cloves garlic, chopped
1	teaspoon ground fennel seeds
	salt and freshly ground pepper
2	cups (16 fl oz/500 ml) water
1	lemon peel strip, about 2 inches (5 cm) long
2	tablespoons fresh lemon juice
	lemon wedges

Fennel is related to a group of herbs including anise, cumin, dill, coriander and caraway. In the vegetable world, however, fennel is recognized as having a taste all its own, one often compared to licorice.

CUT OFF THE STALKS and feathery fronds from the fennel bulbs. Reserve the stalks for another use. Chop enough of the feathery fronds to measure 1 tablespoon and reserve some of the remaining fronds for garnish. Set aside. Remove any damaged outer leaves from the bulbs and discard. Cut each bulb into quarters lengthwise and trim away the tough core portions.

In a large saucepan over medium heat, warm the olive oil. Add the garlic and cook, stirring, for 1 minute; do not brown. Add the fennel quarters and the fennel seeds. Season to taste with salt and pepper. Cook uncovered, stirring occasionally, until the fennel begins to soften, about 5 minutes.

Reduce the heat to medium-low, add the water and lemon peel, cover and cook until the fennel is tender, 20–25 minutes.

Using a slotted spoon, transfer the fennel to a serving platter and keep warm. Raise the heat to high and cook until only ¾ cup (6 fl oz/180 ml) liquid remains, about 5 minutes. Discard the lemon peel. Add the lemon juice, then taste and adjust the seasoning with salt and pepper.

Drizzle the sauce over the fennel and garnish with lemon wedges. Sprinkle with the chopped fennel tops and garnish with the whole fennel fronds. Serve immediately. *Serves 6*

Cauliflower and Broccoli with Roasted Garlic Cloves

2 **small heads garlic, cloves separated and peeled**

2 **tablespoons extra-virgin olive oil**

   salt and freshly ground pepper

1 **head cauliflower, about ¾ lb (375 g), cut into 1½-inch (4-cm) florets**

1 **bunch broccoli, about ¾ lb (375 g), cut into 1½-inch (4-cm) florets**

   lemon wedges

The word *cauliflower* comes from the Italian *cavolo a fiore,* meaning "a cabbage that blooms like a flower," and was regularly grown in the garden plots of ancient Rome. Broccoli was known by the ancient Romans as well, and its name is derived from *bracchium,* meaning "a strong branch." When purchasing broccoli or cauliflower, select those heads that are crisp and smell sweet.

POSITION A RACK in the upper part of an oven and preheat to 400°F (200°C).

Place the garlic cloves in a small baking dish and drizzle with 1 tablespoon of the oil. Season to taste with salt and pepper and toss to coat evenly. Cover with aluminum foil and bake until tender, 20–25 minutes. Remove the foil and continue to bake until lightly golden, 5–10 minutes longer. Remove from the oven and set aside.

Bring a large pot three-fourths full of salted water to a boil. Add the cauliflower and cook until tender when pierced with a fork, 3–5 minutes. Remove with a slotted spoon and transfer to a platter to cool. Repeat with the broccoli, and again transfer to the platter to cool.

In a large frying pan over medium-high heat, warm the remaining 1 tablespoon olive oil. Add the cauliflower and broccoli and cook, stirring occasionally, until warm, about 3 minutes. Add the garlic cloves and toss together until the garlic is warm, about 1 minute. Season to taste with salt and pepper.

Transfer the broccoli, cauliflower and garlic cloves to a warmed serving dish. Garnish with the lemon wedges and serve immediately. *Serves 6*

How simple and frugal a thing is happiness:
a glass of wine, a roast chestnut, a wretched
little brazier, the sound of the sea...

—Nikos Kazantzakis

Brussels Sprouts with Chestnuts

½   **lb (250 g) fresh chestnuts**

1½   **lb (750 g) Brussels sprouts**

2   **tablespoons unsalted butter**

     salt and freshly ground pepper

Brussels sprouts, which resemble miniature cabbages, grow in rows on long stalks. Serve this dish with roast turkey *(recipe on page 66)* or maple-glazed crispy duck *(page 58)*.

USING A SHARP KNIFE, make a small incision across the flat side of each chestnut. Place the chestnuts in a saucepan, add water to cover and place over medium heat. Bring to a simmer, reduce the heat to low and cook until the nut meats can be easily pierced with a knife, 45–55 minutes. Remove from the heat. Using a slotted spoon, remove the chestnuts a few at a time from the hot water (the nuts are easier to peel when hot). Peel away the hard shells and inner sheaths and discard.

Remove any damaged outer leaves from the Brussels sprouts and discard. Bring a large saucepan three-fourths full of water to a boil. Add the Brussels sprouts and simmer, uncovered, until tender, 6–8 minutes. Drain and return to the saucepan. Add the chestnuts and butter and place over medium heat until the butter melts and the chestnuts are hot, about 1 minute. Stir well and season to taste with salt and pepper.

Transfer to a warmed serving dish and serve hot. *Serves 6*

Golden Potato and Mushroom Gratin

½   **oz (15 g) dried wild mush-rooms such as porcini, chanterelle or shiitake**

    boiling water, as needed

8   **potatoes** *(see note),* **1¾–2 lb (875 g–1 kg)**

1½   **tablespoons unsalted butter**

1   **lb (500 g) button mushrooms, brushed clean and thinly sliced**

2   **teaspoons chopped fresh thyme**

    salt and freshly ground pepper

3   **oz (90 g) blue cheese such as Gorgonzola, Stilton, Maytag or Roquefort, at room temperature**

2½   **cups (20 fl oz/625 ml) heavy (double) cream**

½   **cup (2 oz/60 g) freshly grated Parmesan cheese**

The potato has been cultivated for thousands of years and it grows in a multi-tude of shapes, colors, textures and sizes. A number of varieties would work well in this dish: Try Yukon Gold, Yellow Finn, Red, Désirée, Red LaSoda or Pink Blossom. Garnish the gratin with whole fresh wild mushrooms and fresh herb sprigs, if you like.

PLACE THE MUSHROOMS in a small bowl and add boiling water to cover. Let stand for 30 minutes until softened. Drain the mushrooms, chop coarsely and set aside.

Position a rack in the upper part of an oven and preheat to 400°F (200°C). Oil a 3-qt (3-l) gratin dish or other baking dish.

Thinly slice the potatoes and place in a bowl of water to cover until ready to use.

In a large frying pan over high heat, melt the butter. Add the button mushrooms, rehydrated wild mushrooms and thyme and sauté, stirring occa-sionally, until the mushrooms are tender and the liquid they released has com-pletely evaporated, 8–10 minutes. Season to taste with salt and pepper.

In a bowl, mash the blue cheese with the cream until smooth, then season to taste with salt and pepper. Place one-third of the potatoes on the bottom of the baking dish. Layer half of the mushrooms evenly over the potatoes. Add a layer of half of the remaining potatoes, and then a layer of all the remaining mushrooms. Top with the remaining potatoes and pour the cream mixture evenly over the top. Sprinkle evenly with the Parmesan cheese.

Bake until the potatoes are tender and the cream is almost fully absorbed, 40–50 minutes. Serve hot, spooning the gratin directly from the dish. *Serves 6–8*

Mixed-Grain Pilaf with Cranberries and Pine Nuts

½	cup (2½ oz/75 g) pine nuts
1	tablespoon canola or vegetable oil
¾	cup (5 oz/155 g) basmati rice
¼	cup (2 oz/60 g) amaranth
¼	cup (1 oz/30 g) quinoa
¼	cup (2 oz/60 g) millet
½	cup (2 oz/60 g) dried cranberries
¾	teaspoon salt
	freshly ground pepper
2	cups (16 fl oz/500 ml) chicken stock
1	cup (8 fl oz/250 ml) water

Grains have been a symbol of the autumn harvest for centuries, although modern-day cooks have only recently begun to reintroduce themselves to some of the now lesser-known ancient varieties. A wide array of hearty grains—amaranth, quinoa, millet, barley, cornmeal and bulgur—is available in health-food stores. Here, several are combined in an appealing fall pilaf.

IN A FRYING PAN over medium heat, toast the pine nuts, stirring constantly, until lightly golden, 2–3 minutes. Remove from the heat and set aside.

In a saucepan over medium heat, warm the oil. Add the rice, amaranth, quinoa and millet and stir until the grains are coated with the oil and hot, 1–2 minutes. Raise the heat to high and add the cranberries, salt, pepper to taste, stock and water. Bring to a boil, reduce the heat to low, cover and simmer until the grains are tender and the liquid is absorbed, about 25 minutes.

Add the pine nuts and fluff with a fork to mix. Taste and adjust the seasonings. Transfer to a warmed serving dish and serve immediately. *Serves 6*

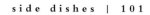

Sweet Potato Oven Fries

2½ **lb (1.25 kg) sweet potatoes, well scrubbed**

3 **tablespoons olive oil**

  salt and freshly ground pepper

1 **teaspoon chopped fresh sage**

1 **clove garlic, minced**

The skin color of sweet potatoes ranges from tan to orange-brown to dark red to purple, while the flesh varies from the creamy white of a popular Japanese variety to the deep orange of more common members of the clan.

POSITION A RACK in the upper part of an oven and preheat to 450°F (230°C).

Trim off the ends from the sweet potatoes. Cut in half lengthwise and place, cut sides down, on a work surface. Using a sharp knife, cut each half lengthwise into wedges ½ inch (12 mm) wide. Place the wedges in a large bowl, drizzle with 2 tablespoons of the olive oil and toss to coat evenly. Season well with salt and pepper.

Place the wedges in a single layer on a large baking sheet, allowing ample space on all sides to ensure even cooking. Bake until golden and tender when pierced with a knife, about 50 minutes.

Remove the baking sheet from the oven and, using a spatula, pile the sweet potatoes in the center of the pan, carefully loosening any that may have stuck to the baking sheet. In a small bowl or cup, combine the remaining 1 tablespoon olive oil, the sage and garlic. Pour over the hot sweet potatoes, toss well to coat and serve immediately. *Serves 6*

desserts

The grim frost is at hand, when the apples will fall thick, almost thunderous, on the hardened earth.

—D.H. Lawrence

Baked Apples with Calvados Custard Sauce

6   **apples such as Golden Delicious, Cortland, Rome Beauty or McIntosh**

½   **cup (4 oz/120 g) firmly packed light brown sugar**

4   **tablespoons (2 oz/60 g) unsalted butter, at room temperature**

½   **cup (4 fl oz/125 ml) water**

½   **teaspoon ground cinnamon**

½   **teaspoon grated lemon zest**

½   **cup (2 oz/60 g) walnuts**

⅓   **cup (1 oz/30 g) dried apples, chopped**

For the custard sauce:

4   **egg yolks**

2   **cups (16 fl oz/500 ml) milk**

¼   **cup (2 oz/60 g) granulated sugar**

¼   **teaspoon vanilla extract (essence)**

2   **tablespoons Calvados or other dry apple brandy**

PREHEAT AN OVEN to 375°F (190°C). Peel the top one-fourth of each apple, leaving the stem intact. Cut a slice ½ inch (12 mm) thick off the stem ends and set aside. Core the apples, cutting to within ½ inch (12 mm) of the base but leaving the base intact.

In a small pan over medium-high heat, combine ¼ cup (2 oz/60 g) of the brown sugar, 2 tablespoons of the butter, the water, ¼ teaspoon of the cinnamon and the lemon zest. Bring to a boil, stirring to dissolve the sugar. Remove the syrup from the heat and set aside.

Spread the walnuts on a baking sheet and toast until lightly golden and fragrant, 5–7 minutes. Let cool, chop coarsely and place in a bowl. Add the dried apples and the remaining ¼ cup (2 oz/60 g) brown sugar, ¼ teaspoon cinnamon and the remaining 2 tablespoons butter. Stir to mix well. Fill the apples with the mixture, dividing it evenly. Replace the stem ends.

Arrange the apples in a 2-qt (2-l) baking dish and pour the syrup over them. Cover and bake until nearly tender, about 30 minutes. Uncover, baste with the pan juices and bake until easily pierced, about 15 minutes longer.

Meanwhile, make the sauce: In a bowl, whisk the egg yolks until blended. In a saucepan over medium-high heat, combine the milk and granulated sugar and heat, stirring until the sugar dissolves. When small bubbles appear along the edges of the pan, slowly whisk the milk mixture into the egg yolks. Pour the mixture back into the pan and return to medium heat. Cook, stirring constantly, just until the mixture thickens and coats the back of a spoon, 3–4 minutes. Immediately remove from the heat and strain through a fine-mesh sieve into a bowl. Stir in the vanilla and brandy. Cover and refrigerate.

Remove the apples from the oven, spoon some of the pan juices over them and slip under a preheated broiler (griller). Broil (grill) until lightly golden, about 1 minute. To serve, spoon the sauce onto individual plates and place an apple in the center. *Serves 6*

Dizzy with light, we dipped into that enormous book of holidays, its pages blazing with sunshine and scented with the sweet melting pulp of golden pears.

—Bruno Schulz

Upside-Down Pear Gingerbread

¾ cup (6 oz/185 g) unsalted butter, at room temperature

1 cup (7 oz/220 g) firmly packed brown sugar

3 Bosc pears, peeled, cored and thinly sliced

1 egg

¼ cup (3 oz/90 g) dark molasses

1½ cups (7½ oz/235 g) all-purpose (plain) flour

2 teaspoons ground ginger

1½ teaspoons ground cinnamon

½ teaspoon baking soda (bicarbonate of soda)

¼ teaspoon freshly grated nutmeg

¼ teaspoon ground cloves

   pinch of salt

⅓ cup (3 fl oz/80 ml) boiling water

Boscs are firm pears particularly well suited to baking, broiling or poaching. Serve the gingerbread with whipped cream or vanilla ice cream, if desired.

PLACE A 9-INCH (23-CM) square cake pan over medium heat, add ¼ cup (2 oz/60 g) of the butter and allow to melt. Add ½ cup (3½ oz/110 g) of the brown sugar and stir just until the sugar melts. Add the pear slices and cook, stirring occasionally, until the pears just begin to soften, about 5 minutes. Arrange the pears in an even layer over the bottom of the pan and remove from the heat.

Preheat an oven to 350°F (180°C).

In a bowl, using an electric mixer set on high speed, beat together the remaining ½ cup (4 oz/125 g) butter and ½ cup (3½ oz/110 g) brown sugar until light, about 3 minutes. Add the egg and molasses and beat until well mixed, about 1 minute. Sift together the flour, ginger, cinnamon, baking soda, nutmeg, cloves and salt into another bowl. Dividing the flour mixture into 2 batches, and using a rubber spatula, fold the flour mixture into the butter-sugar mixture alternately with the water, beginning and ending with the flour. Do not overmix.

Spoon the batter over the pears. Bake until springy to the touch, 30–40 minutes. Remove from the oven and let cool on a rack for about 5 minutes. Carefully invert the cake onto a serving plate. Cut into squares and serve warm or at room temperature. *Serves 9*

*O, it sets my heart a-clickin'
   like the tickin' of a clock,
When the frost is on the punkin
   and the fodder's in the shock.*

—James Whitcomb Riley

Spiced Pumpkin Pie

For the pastry:

1½   cups (7½ oz/235 g) all-purpose (plain) flour

½   teaspoon salt

1   tablespoon sugar

½   cup (4 oz/125 g) unsalted butter, chilled, cut into pieces

3   tablespoons vegetable shortening, chilled, cut into pieces

3   tablespoons ice water

For the filling:

1   small pumpkin, 2½ lb (1.25 kg)

¼   cup (3 oz/90 g) maple syrup

¼   cup (2 oz/60 g) firmly packed light brown sugar

1½   teaspoons ground cinnamon

1   teaspoon ground ginger

½   teaspoon ground nutmeg

¼   teaspoon ground cloves

3   eggs, beaten

¾   cup (6 fl oz/180 ml) half-and-half (half cream)

1   cup (8 fl oz/250 ml) heavy (double) cream

2   tablespoons confectioners' (icing) sugar

½   teaspoon vanilla extract (essence)

TO MAKE THE PASTRY, in a large bowl, mix together the flour, salt and sugar. Make a well in the center, add the butter and shortening and, using your fingertips, rub them into the flour mixture until small, flat pieces form. Sprinkle on the water and gently mix with a fork. Gather the dough into a rough ball; do not overwork. Wrap in plastic wrap and refrigerate for 2 hours.

Preheat an oven to 350°F (180°C). Lightly oil a baking sheet.

To make the filling, cut the pumpkin in half through the stem end and place, cut side down, on the baking sheet. Bake until easily pierced with a knife, about 1 hour. Let cool and, using a spoon, scoop out the seeds and fibers and discard. Spoon the flesh into a food processor fitted with the metal blade. Purée until smooth. Measure out 1½ cups (12 oz/375 g); set aside. Reserve the rest for another use. Raise the oven temperature to 375°F (190°C).

On a well-floured work surface, roll out the dough into a 12-inch (30-cm) round. Transfer the dough to a 9-inch (23-cm) pie pan and gently press into the bottom and sides of the pan. Trim the edges, leaving a ½-inch (12-mm) overhang, then fold under the overhang to make an even edge and crimp to form an attractive rim. Prick the bottom and sides of the pastry with a fork. Place in the freezer for 10 minutes.

Line the pastry with aluminum foil and fill with pie weights. Bake for 15 minutes. Remove the weights and foil and continue to bake until lightly golden, 10–15 minutes longer. Transfer to a rack and let cool.

In a bowl, whisk together the pumpkin purée, maple syrup, brown sugar, cinnamon, ginger, nutmeg, cloves, eggs and half-and-half until well mixed. Pour into the prebaked pie shell. Bake until a skewer inserted into the center comes out clean, 45–55 minutes. Transfer to the rack and let cool for at least 30 minutes before serving.

In a chilled bowl, whisk the cream until soft peaks form. Sift the confectioners' sugar directly on top, add the vanilla and fold in. Serve the pie with the cream on the side. *Makes one 9-inch (23-cm) pie; serves 6–8*

She was stretched on her back beneath the pear tree soaking in the alto chant of the visiting bees...

—Zora Neale Hurston

Warm Caramelized Pears with Clove Zabaglione

Zabaglione is one of Italy's great desserts. The ethereal foamy custard sauce is usually made with egg yolks, sugar and Marsala wine. In this recipe, the addition of golden raisins and spices gives it a festive flavor.

PREHEAT AN OVEN to 350°F (180°C).

To prepare the pears, in a small bowl, stir together the cloves, allspice, cinnamon and nutmeg. In a small saucepan over medium heat, combine the Marsala, honey, butter, lemon zest and half of the mixed spices and heat just until the butter melts. Remove from the heat. (Reserve the remaining spices for adding to the zabaglione.) Place the pears in a baking dish, hollow side down, and pour the Marsala mixture over them.

Bake the pears, basting occasionally with the liquid in the dish and turning them over halfway through cooking, until easily pierced with a knife, 30–40 minutes. Remove from the oven and keep warm.

Meanwhile, prepare for the zabaglione: Place the raisins and half of the Marsala in a small saucepan over high heat. Bring to a boil and immediately remove from the heat. Let stand until cool, about 30 minutes.

About 15 minutes before serving, bring a saucepan half full of water to a gentle simmer. Using a whisk or handheld electric mixer, beat together the egg yolks, sugar and water in a large heatproof bowl. Whisk in the remaining Marsala and set the bowl over the pan of barely simmering water. Do not allow the water to touch the bowl. Whisk constantly until the mixture is thick, frothy, begins to hold soft peaks and no liquid remains at the bottom of the bowl, about 10 minutes. Drain the raisins and discard the Marsala. Fold the raisins and the reserved spices into the zabaglione.

To serve, place 2 pear halves in each individual bowl. Spoon the zabaglione onto the pears, distributing it evenly. Serve immediately. *Serves 6*

For the pears:

½ teaspoon ground cloves

¼ teaspoon ground allspice

¼ teaspoon ground cinnamon

⅛ teaspoon freshly grated nutmeg

½ cup (4 fl oz/125 ml) sweet Marsala wine

3 tablespoons honey

1½ tablespoons unsalted butter

2 lemon zest strips, each 3 inches (7.5 cm) long and ½ inch (12 mm) wide

6 Bosc or French Butter pears, peeled, halved with stems intact and cored

For the zabaglione:

⅓ cup (2 oz/60 g) golden raisins (sultanas)

¾ cup (6 fl oz/180 ml) sweet Marsala wine

4 egg yolks

¼ cup (2 oz/60 g) sugar

2 tablespoons water

Poached Quince Tart

2½ **cups (20 fl oz/625 ml) dry red wine such as Barolo, Cabernet Sauvignon or Côtes-du-Rhône**

¼ **cup (2 oz/60 g) sugar**

8 **whole cloves**

3 **lemon zest strips, each about 2 inches (5 cm) long and ½ inch (12 mm) wide**

2 **cinnamon sticks**

2½ **lb (1.25 kg) quinces, peeled, halved, cored and cut into thin slices**

For the pastry:

⅔ **cup (5 oz/155 g) unsalted butter, at room temperature**

¾ **cup (6 oz/185 g) sugar**

3 **egg yolks**

1½ **cups (7½ oz/235 g) all-purpose (plain) flour, or as needed**

⅔ **cup (4 oz/125 g) polenta**

½ **teaspoon salt**

1 **cup (8 fl oz/250 ml) heavy cream**

IN A LARGE SAUCEPAN over medium-high heat, combine the wine, sugar, cloves, lemon zest and cinnamon sticks. Bring to a boil and boil until reduced to 2 cups (16 fl oz/500 ml), about 15 minutes. Add the quince slices, reduce the heat to medium-low and cook uncovered, gently pushing the slices under the liquid from time to time, until tender, 1–1½ hours.

Remove from the heat and strain through a fine-mesh sieve into a bowl; discard the cloves and lemon zest and reserve the liquid. Place the quince slices on paper towels and let cool. Return the liquid to the pan and boil over high heat until only ½ cup (4 fl oz/125 ml) thick syrup remains.

To make the pastry, in a food processor fitted with the metal blade, combine the butter and sugar and process until light in color, 2–3 minutes. With the processor on, add the egg yolks one at a time. Sift together the 1½ cups (7½ oz/235 g) flour, polenta and salt directly over the creamed mixture and process until the mixture comes together to form a dough, about 1 minute. Add additional flour, 1 tablespoon at a time, if the dough is sticky. Wrap the dough in plastic wrap and refrigerate for 30 minutes.

Preheat an oven to 375°F (190°C). Cut the dough in half and return half to the refrigerator. Using your fingers, press the other half of the dough evenly over the bottom and sides of a tart pan 9 inches (23 cm) in diameter with a removable bottom. Place the drained quince slices in the tart shell. On a lightly floured work surface, roll out the remaining dough ¼ inch (6 mm) thick. Using a heart-shaped cookie cutter 2½ inches (6 cm) across at its widest point, cut out as many hearts as possible. Place the hearts on top of the quince slices, starting near the rim and with the widest part of each heart facing toward the edge. Overlap the hearts slightly and cover the top completely. Bake until golden brown, about 40 minutes. Transfer to a rack and let cool.

In a bowl, whisk the cream until soft peaks form. Fold in 1 tablespoon of the reduced poaching liquid; reserve the remaining liquid for another use. Serve the tart with the cream on the side. *Makes one 9-inch (23-cm) tart; serves 8*

There's nought, no doubt, so much the spirit calms
As rum and true religion.

—Lord Byron

Rum Raisin Ice Cream with Cider Sauce

For the ice cream:

½ cup (3 oz/90 g) dark raisins

½ cup (4 fl oz/125 ml) dark rum

8 egg yolks

¾ cup (6 oz/185 g) firmly packed light brown sugar

1¾ cups (14 fl oz/440 ml) milk

1¾ cups (14 fl oz/440 ml) heavy (double) cream

½ teaspoon vanilla extract (essence)

For the sauce:

3 cups (24 fl oz/750 ml) apple cider

2 tablespoons dark brown sugar

2 teaspoons cornstarch (cornflour)

1 cinnamon stick

¼ teaspoon freshly grated nutmeg

½ cup (3 oz/90 g) golden raisins (sultanas)

1 tablespoon unsalted butter

To make the ice cream, in a saucepan over medium heat, combine the raisins and rum and heat until bubbling around the edges, about 2 minutes. Remove from the heat, transfer to a bowl and let cool, 30–40 minutes. In the same saucepan off the heat, stir together the egg yolks and sugar.

In another saucepan, combine the milk and cream. Place over medium heat until bubbles form around the edges of the pan, about 5 minutes. Remove from the heat and slowly add to the yolk-sugar mixture, whisking constantly. Place over medium heat and cook, stirring constantly with a wooden spoon, just until the mixture begins to thicken and coats the back of a spoon, 2–3 minutes. Immediately remove from the heat and strain through a fine-mesh sieve into a bowl. Add the vanilla. Strain the raisins over a small bowl and add ¼ cup (2 fl oz/60 ml) of the rum to the custard base; reserve any remaining rum for the sauce. Set the raisins aside. Whisk the ice cream base for 1 minute to cool, then cover and chill well, about 2 hours.

Meanwhile, make the sauce: In a small bowl, whisk together ½ cup (4 fl oz/125 ml) of the cider, the brown sugar and cornstarch. Pour into a saucepan and add the remaining 2½ cups (20 fl oz/625 ml) cider, the cinnamon stick, nutmeg and golden raisins and mix well. Bring to a boil over high heat. Reduce the heat to medium-high and simmer, uncovered, until only 1½ cups (12 fl oz/375 ml) remain, 10–15 minutes. Remove from the heat and discard the cinnamon stick. Stir in the butter and the reserved rum. Set aside.

Transfer the ice cream base to an ice cream maker and freeze according to the manufacturer's directions. Add the reserved raisins during the final few minutes of churning.

To serve, reheat the cider sauce. Scoop the ice cream into bowls and drizzle with the sauce. *Makes about 1½ qt (1.5 l); serves 6–8*

If you tell me that you desire a fig,
I answer you that there must be time.
Let it first blossom, then bear fruit, then ripen.

—Epictetus

Fig and Walnut Tartlets

For the short-crust pastry:

1   cup (5 oz/155 g) all-purpose (plain) flour

1   tablespoon granulated sugar

    pinch of salt

½   cup (4 fl oz/125 g) butter, out of the refrigerator for 15 minutes, cut into pieces

1–3 teaspoons water

For the filling:

1   cup (4 oz/125 g) walnuts

⅓   cup (1½ oz/45 g) confectioners' (icing) sugar

2   tablespoons all-purpose (plain) flour

1½ tablespoons unsalted butter

1   egg

1   tablespoon brandy

1   teaspoon grated orange zest

9   fresh figs such as Mission or Kadota

1   cup (8 fl oz/250 ml) heavy (double) cream

1½ tablespoons confectioners' (icing) sugar, plus sugar for dusting

1   teaspoon vanilla extract (essence)

    orange zest strips and walnut halves for garnish, optional

PREHEAT AN OVEN to 375°F (190°C).

To make the pastry, in a food processor fitted with the metal blade, combine the flour, 1 tablespoon sugar and the salt. Pulse just to mix. Add the butter and pulse until the mixture resembles coarse meal. With the motor running, add just enough water for the mixture to come together into a rough mass. Gather the dough into a ball and flatten into a disk 6 inches (15 cm) in diameter. Wrap in plastic wrap and refrigerate for 30 minutes.

To make the filling, spread the walnuts on a baking sheet and toast until lightly golden and fragrant, 5–7 minutes. Let cool. In the food processor fitted with the metal blade, process the walnuts and half of the confectioners' sugar until finely ground, 30–60 seconds. Sift together the remaining confectioners' sugar and flour directly onto the nuts and pulse several times to mix. Add the butter, egg, brandy and orange zest and pulse until blended. Transfer to a bowl. Finely chop 4 of the figs and add to the bowl. Stir gently until well mixed.

Divide the dough into 8 equal portions. Gently press each portion into an individual tart pan 3 inches (7.5 cm) in diameter, building up the sides slightly. Place the lined pans in the freezer for 15 minutes.

Raise the oven temperature to 400°F (200°C). Place the tart pans on a baking sheet and bake until golden, about 15 minutes.

Meanwhile, cut the remaining 5 figs into slices ¼ inch (6 mm) thick. When the tart shells are ready, remove from the oven and pour the batter into them, dividing it evenly. Top each tart with an equal amount of the sliced figs and return them to the oven. Bake until set and the tops are golden, about 35 minutes.

While the tarts are baking, in a bowl, beat the cream until soft peaks form. Sift the 1½ tablespoons confectioners' sugar directly on top and add the vanilla. Fold in just until mixed. Remove the tartlets from the oven and, if desired, garnish with orange zest strips and walnut halves. Dust with confectioners' sugar and serve immediately with the cream on the side. *Serves 8*

For the pastry:

2½ cups (12½ oz/390 g) all-
    purpose (plain) flour

1   teaspoon salt

2   tablespoons sugar

10 tablespoons (5 oz/155 g)
    unsalted butter, chilled,
    cut into pieces

10 tablespoons (5 oz/155 g)
    vegetable shortening, chilled,
    cut into pieces

7   tablespoons (3½ fl oz/105 ml)
    ice water

1   teaspoon distilled white
    vinegar

For the filling:

2½ lb (1.25 kg) baking apples,
    peeled, quartered, cored and
    cut lengthwise into slices ½
    inch (12 mm) thick

½   cup (4 oz/125 g) sugar, or
    as needed

½   teaspoon ground cinnamon

¼   teaspoon ground nutmeg

1   tablespoon fresh lemon juice

2   tablespoons unsalted butter,
    cut into pieces

1   egg yolk

1   tablespoon heavy (double)
    cream

Old-Fashioned Apple Pie

Laying a slice of Cheddar cheese atop a wedge of warm apple pie is an American tradition. Today a scoop of vanilla ice cream is generally preferred.

TO MAKE THE PASTRY, in a large bowl, mix together the flour, salt and sugar. Make a well in the center, add the butter and shortening and, using your fingertips, rub them into the flour mixture until small, flat pieces form. Combine the water and vinegar and, using a fork, gently mix just enough of the liquid into the flour mixture for it to come together in a rough ball; do not overwork. Discard the remaining liquid. Divide the dough in half and wrap each half in plastic wrap. Refrigerate for 2 hours.

To make the filling, in a bowl, toss together the apples, sugar (adding more to taste if the apples are tart), cinnamon, nutmeg and lemon juice.

Preheat an oven to 400°F (200°C).

On a lightly floured work surface, roll out half of the dough (leave the other half refrigerated) into a round 12 inches (30 cm) in diameter. Fold the dough in half and then into quarters and transfer it to a 9-inch (23-cm) pie pan. Unfold and gently press into the pan. Trim the edges even with the rim. Roll out the remaining dough into a 10-inch (25-cm) round.

Turn the apples into the pastry-lined pan, mounding them slightly in the center. Dot evenly with the butter. Brush the edges of the dough with water. Fold the dough round into quarters and unfold over the apples. Press together the top and bottom crusts to seal, then trim the edges flush with the pan rim and crimp to form an attractive edge. Cut the pastry scraps into decorative shapes and arrange on top, if desired. In a small bowl, beat together the egg yolk and cream and brush over the pastry. Make a few slits near the center to allow steam to escape.

Bake for 25 minutes. Reduce the heat to 350°F (180°C) and continue to bake until the apples are tender (insert a knife blade through a slit) and the top is golden brown, 15–20 minutes. Transfer to a rack and let cool for at least 20 minutes before serving. *Makes one 9-inch (23-cm) pie; serves 8*

And joined in love together,
The Thistle, Shamrock, Rose entwine
The Maple leaf forever!

—Alexander Muir

Maple Leaf Cookies

¾ **cup (6 oz/185 g) sugar, plus sugar for dusting**

1 **cup (8 oz/250 g) unsalted butter, at room temperature**

½ **cup (5½ oz/170 g) pure maple syrup**

1 **teaspoon vanilla extract (essence)**

1 **egg yolk**

3 **cups (15 oz/470 g) all-purpose (plain) flour**

¼ **teaspoon salt**

These cookies are inspired by the changing colors of maple leaves in autumn. The dough can be made up to several days ahead, well wrapped and stored in the refrigerator until ready to bake. Serve the cookies with the rum raisin ice cream with cider sauce *(recipe on page 117)*.

IN A BOWL, using an electric mixer set on high speed, beat together the ¾ cup (6 oz/185 g) sugar and the butter until light and fluffy, about 3 minutes. Add the maple syrup, vanilla and egg yolk and mix well for 1 minute. Sift together the flour and salt directly onto the butter mixture, then beat on medium speed until well combined, about 2 minutes. Shape the dough into a ball, wrap in plastic wrap and refrigerate overnight.

The next day, preheat an oven to 350°F (180°C). Lightly butter 2 baking sheets.

Divide the dough into 2 equal portions. Working with 1 portion at a time, place the dough on a lightly floured work surface and, using a rolling pin, roll out ⅛ inch (3 mm) thick. Using a maple leaf–shaped cookie cutter 4 inches (10 cm) across at the widest part, cut out as many cookies as possible. As the cookies are cut, place them 1 inch (2.5 cm) apart on a prepared baking sheet. Then, using a small paring knife, mark each cutout in a pattern resembling the veins of a maple leaf. Gather up the scraps, reroll and cut out as many additional cookies as possible. Repeat with the second dough portion, placing them on the second prepared baking sheet. Dust each cookie with about ½ teaspoon sugar.

Place the baking sheets on separate racks in the oven and bake the cookies until the edges are lightly golden, 10–12 minutes, switching the pans and rotating them 180 degrees halfway through baking. Remove from the oven and transfer to a rack to cool. Store in an airtight container at room temperature for up to 4 days. *Makes 2–2½ dozen*

1   cup (8 oz/250 g) sugar

⅓   cup (3 fl oz/80 ml) plus ¼ cup (2 fl oz/60 ml) water

1½   cups (12 fl oz/375 ml) heavy (double) cream

1½   cups (12 fl oz/375 ml) milk

8   egg yolks

     boiling water, as needed

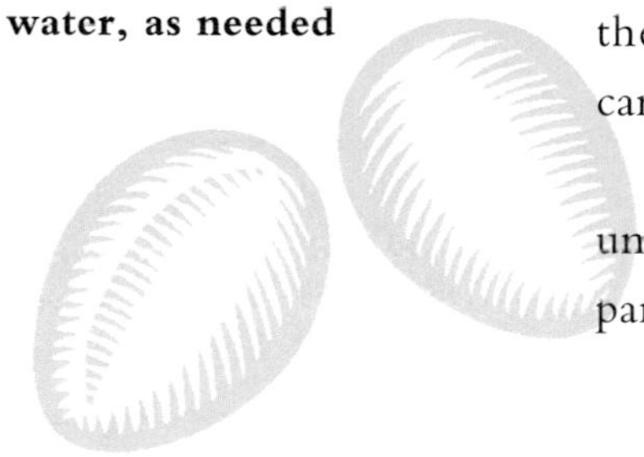

Caramel Pots de Crème

This smooth, creamy custard dessert flavored with bittersweet caramel is one of the cold-weather comfort foods that people crave during the autumn months. Garnish each serving with a dollop of whipped cream and toasted walnuts or pecans.

PLACE THE SUGAR and the ⅓ cup (3 fl oz/80 ml) water in a heavy saucepan over medium-high heat. Cover and bring to a boil. Uncover and cook until the sugar turns golden amber in color, 8–12 minutes. Be careful, as the caramel is very hot.

Meanwhile, combine the cream and milk in a large saucepan over medium-high heat and warm until small bubbles appear along the edges of the pan. Remove from the heat.

Preheat an oven to 325°F (165°C).

When the caramel is ready, add the remaining ¼ cup (2 fl oz/60 ml) water and whisk vigorously until the bubbles subside. Pour the caramel into the hot cream mixture and whisk together until mixed. Let cool for about 10 minutes.

In a bowl, whisk together the egg yolks. Slowly add the caramel mixture to the egg yolks, stirring constantly with a wooden spoon until mixed. Strain through a fine-mesh sieve into a pitcher.

Pour the custard into six ⅔-cup (5 fl oz/160-ml) ramekins. Place the ramekins in a baking pan. Pour boiling water into the pan to reach about 1 inch (2.5 cm) up the sides of the ramekins. Bake until the edges of the custards are set, 40–50 minutes. Remove the baking pan from the oven and transfer to a rack to cool for 10 minutes.

Remove the custards from the water bath and let cool. Refrigerate for several hours or overnight until well chilled. Serve chilled or at room temperature. *Serves 6*

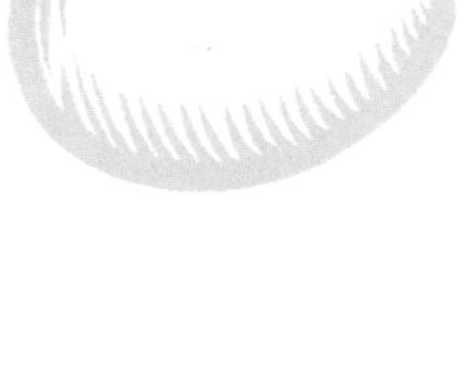

Rise in the heart, and gather to the eyes,
In looking on the happy autumn fields,
And thinking of the days that are no more.

—Alfred Lord Tennyson

Caramelized Nut Tart

For the short-crust pastry:

1½ cups (7½ oz/235 g) all-purpose (plain) flour

1½ tablespoons sugar

pinch of salt

¾ cup (6 oz/185 g) unsalted butter, out of the refrigerator for 15 minutes, cut into pieces

about 1½ tablespoons water

For the filling:

½ teaspoon baking soda (bicarbonate of soda)

¼ cup (1¼ oz/37 g) hazelnuts (filberts)

¼ cup (1 oz/30 g) sliced (flaked) almonds

¼ cup (1 oz/30 g) chopped walnuts

¼ cup (1 oz/30 g) chopped pecans

¾ cup (6 fl oz/180 ml) heavy (double) cream

¾ cup (6 oz/185 g) sugar

½ teaspoon vanilla extract (essence)

To MAKE THE PASTRY, in a food processor fitted with the metal blade, combine the flour, sugar and salt. Pulse just to mix. Add the butter and pulse until the mixture resembles coarse meal. With the motor running, add water as needed for the mixture to come together in a rough mass. Gather the dough into a ball and flatten into a disk 6 inches (15 cm) in diameter. Wrap in plastic wrap and refrigerate for 30 minutes.

Gently press the pastry into the bottom and sides of a 9-inch (23-cm) tart pan with a removable bottom, forming an even layer on the bottom and building up the sides slightly. Place the shell in the freezer for 30 minutes.

Preheat an oven to 400°F (200°C).

Line the pastry with aluminum foil and fill with pie weights. Bake for 10 minutes. Remove the weights and the foil and reduce the temperature to 375°F (190°C). Continue to bake until lightly golden, 15–20 minutes longer. Transfer to a rack and let cool. Leave the oven set at 375°F (190°C).

To make the filling, fill a small saucepan half full of water, add the baking soda and bring to a boil. Add the hazelnuts and boil for 30 seconds. Drain, immediately place in a kitchen towel and rub to remove the skins. Chop the hazelnuts coarsely. Spread the hazelnuts, almonds, walnuts and pecans on a baking sheet and bake until the almonds are lightly golden, 3–5 minutes. Remove from the oven and set aside. Position a rack in the upper part of the oven and raise the temperature to 400°F (200°C).

In a saucepan over medium-high heat, combine the cream, sugar and vanilla extract. Bring to a boil and boil until slightly thickened, about 3 minutes. Remove from the heat and stir in all the nuts. Let stand for 15 minutes.

Pour the filling into the prebaked tart shell and place on a baking sheet. Bake until the top is a combination of creamy white and russet-caramel in color and is dotted all over with small holes, 30–35 minutes. Let cool on a rack for 15 minutes, remove the pan sides and slide the tart onto a serving plate. Serve at room temperature. *Serves 8*

index

acknowledgments

The following kindly lent props for photography: The Gardener, Berkeley, CA; Fillamento, San Francisco, CA;
American Rag, San Francisco, CA; Table Prop, San Francisco, CA; Missy Pepper; Chuck Williams; Williams-Sonoma and Pottery Barn.
The publishers would also like to thank Sarah Lemas and Ken DellaPenta for their editorial assistance.
Thanks also goes to Penina and Michelle Syracuse for surfaces used in photography, and to Lisa Atwood,
Tosha Prysi, Alanna Brady, Jean Tenanes and Paul Weir for their support to the author.